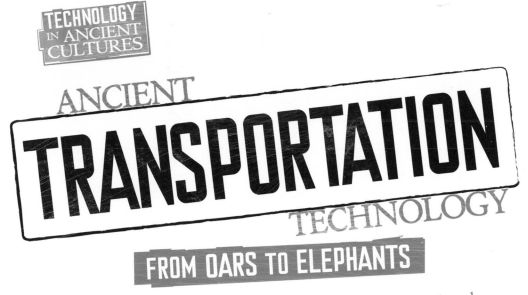

TECHNOLOGY IN ANCIENT CULTURES

ANCIENT **TRANSPORTATION** TECHNOLOGY

FROM OARS TO ELEPHANTS

Michael Woods and
Mary B. Woods

TF
CB

Twenty-First Century Books · Minneapolis

To Jeremy and Matthew

Twenty-First Century Books
A division of Lerner Publishing Group, Inc.
241 First Avenue North
Minneapolis, MN 55401 U.S.A.

Website address: www.lernerbooks.com

Library of Congress Cataloging-in-Publication Data

Woods, Michael, 1946–
        Ancient transportation technology : from oars to elephants / by Michael Woods and Mary B. Woods.
            p.   cm. – (Technology in ancient cultures)
        Includes bibliographical references and index.
        ISBN 978-0-7613-6524-2 (lib. bdg. : alk. paper)
        1. Transportation engineering–History–To 1500–Juvenile literature. 2. Travel–History–To 1500–Juvenile literature. I. Woods, Mary B. (Mary Boyle), 1946– II. Title.
    TA1149.W665 2011
    629.04093--dc22   2010025522

Manufactured in the United States of America
1 – PC – 12/31/10

TABLE OF CONTENTS

4   INTRODUCTION

8   CHAPTER ONE
TRANSPORTATION BASICS

18   CHAPTER TWO
THE ANCIENT MIDDLE EAST

28   CHAPTER THREE
ANCIENT EGYPT

36   CHAPTER FOUR
ANCIENT INDIA

44   CHAPTER FIVE
ANCIENT CHINA

52   CHAPTER SIX
THE ANCIENT AMERICAS

60   CHAPTER SEVEN
ANCIENT GREECE

70   CHAPTER EIGHT
ANCIENT ROME

78   EPILOGUE
AFTER THE ANCIENTS

84   Timeline   91   Further Reading
86   Glossary   93   Websites
88   Source Notes   94   Index
90   Selected Bibliography

THE ANCIENT WORLDS OF TRANSPORTATION

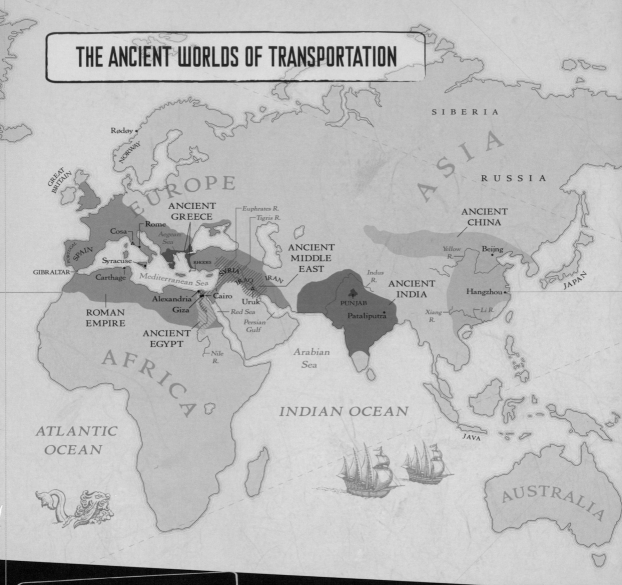

Rødøy • NORWAY · GREAT BRITAIN · PORTUGAL · SPAIN · GIBRALTAR · EUROPE · Cosa · Rome · Aegean Sea · Syracuse · Carthage · ROMAN EMPIRE · Mediterranean Sea · RHODES · ANCIENT GREECE · Alexandria · Cairo · Giza · ANCIENT EGYPT · Nile R. · Red Sea · SYRIA · IRAQ · Uruk · Euphrates R. · Tigris R. · IRAN · ANCIENT MIDDLE EAST · Persian Gulf · AFRICA · ATLANTIC OCEAN · ASIA · SIBERIA · RUSSIA · ANCIENT CHINA · Yellow R. · Beijing · Hangzhou · JAPAN · Indus R. · ANCIENT INDIA · PUNJAB · Pataliputra · Xiang R. · Li R. · Arabian Sea · INDIAN OCEAN · JAVA · AUSTRALIA

INTRODUCTION

What do you think of when you hear the word *technology*? You probably think of something totally new. You might think of research laboratories filled with computers, powerful microscopes, and other scientific tools. But technology doesn't refer to just brand-new machines and discoveries. Technology is as old as human society.

ANCIENT INDIA
ROMAN EMPIRE
ANCIENT GREECE
MESOAMERICA
ANCIENT CHINA
ANCIENT EGYPT
ANCIENT MIDDLE EAST
INCA EMPIRE

♣ Ancient Site
•   City
⌂ Mountains

Technology is the use of knowledge, inventions, and discoveries to make life better. The word *technology* comes from two Greek words. One, *techne*, means "art" or "craft." The other, *logos*, means "logic" or "reason." Ancient Greeks originally used the word *technology* to mean a discussion of arts and crafts. But in modern times, technology usually refers to the craft, the technique, or the tool itself.

There are many forms of technology. Medicine is one form. Agriculture and machinery are others. This book looks at yet another kind of technology—one that has been improving human society for millions of years. That technology is transportation.

Transportation, the movement of people and goods, has always been greatly important to human life. People have used different methods of transportation to escape enemies, send messages to one another, and reach new and better living places. When we think of transportation, we often think of ships, airplanes, or cars. But transportation technology includes more than just vehicles. Maps, ports, lighthouses, and bridges are all part of transportation technology.

ANCIENT ROOTS

You've probably heard people remark, "There's nothing new under the sun!" That's often true in regard to transportation. Modern engineers and scientists rarely make totally new advances in transportation technology. Engineers might figure out how to make roads last longer, wheels turn faster, or bridges span greater distances. But many times, these accomplishments improve on techniques developed by earlier peoples. For example, the sides of modern superhighways slope downward from the center to allow water to drain off. This system is based on an ancient Roman design.

Transportation technology spread across cultures during ancient times. The Phoenicians lived on the eastern shore of the Mediterranean Sea in modern-day Syria and Lebanon. They were the master shipbuilders of the ancient world. With their well-made ships, Phoenician sailors traveled from their ports in the Middle East across and beyond the Mediterranean. Through trade with other cultures, the Phoenicians spread knowledge and ideas.

The ancient Greeks adopted a lot of Phoenician shipbuilding technology. The Greeks traded with the Romans. Roman ships came to resemble Greek vessels, which resembled those of the Phoenicians. Although each group

▲ This stone relief from the ancient city of Sidon in Phoenicia shows a Middle Eastern ship from the first century A.D. Phoenicians were master shipbuilders in ancient times.

added improvements, the basic Mediterranean ship in the ancient world was based on Phoenician designs.

LEARNING FROM THE PAST

Ancient cultures left us a rich legacy of transportation technology. Archaeologists, scientists who study the remains of past cultures, continue to make new discoveries about the history of human transportation. Many tools and vehicles belonging to ancient cultures have decayed, sunk in the ocean, or been buried under layers of earth. Archaeologists often have to piece together clues to guess how ancient vehicles looked and operated. But in some cases, ancient people wrote about tools and vehicles or made pictures of them. So even if a vehicle is gone, modern archaeologists might still know a lot about it.

This book reveals how advances in transportation technology improved ancient life. Read on and discover many amazing techniques that helped move the world forward.

CHAPTER ONE

TRANSPORTATION BASICS

The first humans on Earth lived about 2.5 million years ago. They were hunters and gatherers. They lived in small groups and got their food by hunting game, fishing, and gathering wild plants. When the food in one area was all used up, a group moved to a new place. Hunter-gatherers made tools from stone, wood, animal bones, plant fibers, and clay. In some places on Earth, the hunter-gatherer lifestyle remained unchanged until only a few centuries ago.

Hunter-gatherers traveled constantly. They followed herds of animals. They killed animals for meat, furs, bones, and other materials. Natural disasters such as droughts, wildfires, volcanic eruptions, and climate changes also forced ancient peoples to move.

▼ Early peoples were hunters and gatherers. They followed herds of animals for food. This rock art from present-day eastern South Africa was created by the San, a group of hunter-gatherers who have lived in southern Africa for more than four thousand years.

Speed was important. Hunters who killed an elk had to bring it back to their camp before other animals stole it. Sometimes hunter-gatherers had to move quickly to escape enemies. Transportation was a matter of life and death.

Early peoples had few possessions. But they probably traveled with blankets and stone tools. People with the most efficient ways of carrying heavy loads were most likely to survive.

ANCIENT FOOTWEAR

The foot is humankind's oldest means of transportation. People walked before they used any transportation technology. Improvements in foot travel usually result from improvements in footwear. The very first humans had no footwear. Traveling barefoot for long distances or over rough surfaces would have been hard on these peoples' feet. So people invented shoes. The first foot coverings were much more basic than the shoes of modern times. But they were still a great advance over bare feet. Shoes and sandals enabled people to travel farther, in colder weather, and over rougher terrain.

Archaeologists believe that early peoples in cold regions of Asia and Europe made the first foot coverings. These coverings were probably animal skins that protected feet against cold and snow. People quickly realized that the skins also made walking more comfortable.

Ancient peoples later developed many varieties of warm-weather footwear. Egyptian wall paintings show people wearing sandals with soles made from papyrus plants. Men and women in ancient Japan wore shoes with carved wooden soles, fastened to the

▼ This Egyptian sandal dates from the fourteenth century B.C. It is made of plant fiber.

feet with vines or ropes. In the ancient Middle East, shoemakers added thick leather soles for rough terrain and laces to keep shoes fastened.

Men in ancient Greece wore tough leather boots in battle and while hunting. Greek women and girls sometimes wore ankle-height boots. People in ancient Rome wore light sandals called *solea*, ankle-height leather shoes called *calcei*, and several other styles. For long marches, Roman soldiers wore *caligae*—heavy, high-topped boots. The soles were studded with short, large-headed nails called hobnails. The boots had open toes for ventilation. Open toes also allowed the inside of shoes to dry rapidly after marches in wet weather.

Despite advances in footwear during ancient times, most of the world went barefoot for many centuries. Like a lot of new technology, shoes were expensive. In some cultures, they were available only to the rich, the military, or both. In A.D. 2010, researchers working in modern-day Armenia discovered the world's oldest known leather shoe. The researchers estimate the shoe to be fifty-five hundred years old. It most likely belonged to a person of high status.

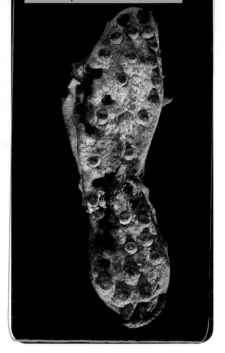

▼ This leather sandal from ancient Rome has a nail-studded sole. The heavy sole held up on rugged land and allowed soldiers to stamp enemies in battle.

THE FIRST BOATS

Early peoples surely noticed tree trunks floating down rivers. After floods, people probably saw birds, raccoons, and other animals clinging to floating logs. The animals traveled rapidly and effortlessly downstream. Eventually, people also clung to logs, kicking with their feet and paddling with their hands. Others grabbed floating objects to keep from drowning. These simple floats were the first boats. Later, people began to lash logs together to make rafts. Bundled logs are more stable than individual logs and can carry heavier loads.

Hunter-gatherers made the first dugout canoes. They used tools such as sharp rocks to hollow out logs. Ancient peoples in Europe, Africa, and North America all relied on this method of boat making. Dugout canoes are still used throughout much of rural Africa. In 1964 archaeologists on England's southern coast discovered a dugout canoe that was 33 feet (10 meters) long and an estimated twenty-two hundred years old.

Australian aborigines, the modern descendants of Australia's earliest residents, traveled by bark boat as late as the early twentieth century. These bark boats were a simple but effective means of transportation. To construct the crafts, aboriginal boatbuilders cut big strips of bark from trees. At the ends of the boats, they sealed the bark strips together with clay. Archaeologists believe ancient aborigines used the same technique thousands of years ago.

▼ Ancient peoples in the midwestern part of North America used dugout canoes like this one. The canoes were made from hollowed-out logs.

LONG VOYAGES

Archaeologists are not sure when or in what area the first long-distance sea voyage occurred. But they have found strong evidence that long-distance boat travel took place at least 130,000 years ago and perhaps thousands of years before then. In 2009 archaeologists discovered multiple ancient stone tools on the Greek island of Crete. They estimate the tools to be anywhere from 130,000 to 700,000 years old. They believe the people who used the tools may have traveled there by boat from mainland Europe.

In modern-day Japan, archaeologists have found stone tools that are roughly one hundred thousand years old. Japan is a group of islands. To reach this group of islands, early peoples must have traveled by boat from the coast of mainland Asia to Japan. They traveled approximately 100 miles (160 kilometers) across the ocean.

Archaeologists have also discovered fifty-thousand-year-old stone tools in the desert of central Australia. Australia is surrounded by water. To reach the continent, early peoples must have floated thousands of miles across the Indian Ocean or Pacific Ocean. They probably stopped at many islands along the way.

THE FIRST BRIDGES

Hunter-gatherers on the move needed convenient ways to cross natural barriers such as rivers and ravines. They needed bridges. The first bridges formed naturally. Natural forces such as lightning and wind often sent trees crashing to the ground. Occasionally, a tree fell in just the right position to allow people to walk on it to cross a river.

The first bridge builder was the first person to deliberately cut down a tree or position a log to span a narrow stream. People realized they could cross wider streams by placing tree trunks end to end, with a rock in midstream for support. Early peoples may also have built bridges out of large flat stones placed across streams.

A WELL-TROD ROAD

The very first roads were paths of packed earth. Deer, elk, and other creatures trampled them down as they repeatedly took the same route to watering spots. Early peoples made roads in the same way—with their own feet.

In 1970 a laborer named Ray Sweet discovered the remains of an elevated walkway in southwestern England while digging in a peat bog. Archaeologists estimate that builders created the walkway in 3807 or 3806 B.C. The bog's soil partially preserved the walkway over time. The road is known as the Sweet Track. It measures about 9,843 feet (3,000 m) in length.

The Sweet Track consisted of crisscrossing tree branches hammered into soft soil. The road's upper branches extended above ground level. Using stone tools, builders split planks from tree trunks. They laid the planks over areas where the upper arms intersected. People walked along a pathway formed by the overlapping planks.

Later research around the Sweet Track revealed that builders laid this road over an even older pathway. The Post Track followed roughly the same route as the Sweet Track. The wooden planks that form the Post Track date a few decades earlier, around 3838 B.C. It is also shorter than the Sweet Track, measuring about 6,562 feet (2,000 m) long. Archaeologists think it may be the first road actually built rather than trampled.

▼ This section of the Sweet Track in England has been moved to a museum. Builders created the walkway in the fourth millenium B.C. to cross wet, boggy terrain.

These roads apparently allowed people to walk through a low, swampy area. The swamps probably supplied people with fish, deer, wild pigs, and other animals, as well as reeds for building huts.

HEAVY LOADS

Hunters probably dreaded the work of transporting a heavy, dead animal back to camp. Archaeologists believe that early hunters used a simple device called a yoke to carry awkward loads.

A yoke was simply a branch cut from a tree. A hunter fastened small game to one end of the branch. He held the other end on his shoulder. To carry more than one load at a time, a hunter balanced a pole over his shoulder, with loads fastened on each end. Two hunters also could tie a large carcass onto a yoke and each carry one end.

The yoke led to the development of another load-bearing vehicle, the travois. A travois consisted of two long poles bound together at an angle. A platform often lay between the poles to support a load. The first travois may have been a forked tree branch with a load placed on the forked portion. People pulled the other end of the branch by hand or perhaps fastened the end to someone's waist. The loaded end simply dragged along the ground. Even the simplest travois enabled people to carry heavy loads farther than ever before.

SKIS AND SLEDGES

Archaeologists long assumed that early peoples used skis for winter travel in cold areas of Asia and Europe. Wood is abundant in these areas. Skis, made of long flat boards, can glide easily over snow. But wood rots quickly. For a long time, archaeologists had no physical evidence of ancient ski use.

In 1964 Russian archaeologists discovered the remains of a ski preserved in a peat bog in northeastern Russia. Laboratory analysis of the wood indicated that the ski was made around 6000 B.C.

One of the oldest-known pictures of a skier is carved on a rock wall in Rødøy, Norway. The forty-five-hundred-year-old carving shows a skier using a single pole to push himself forward. The skis were probably 10 feet (3 m) long. Early ski makers probably recognized that long skis improve stability. The Rødøy Man, as historians call him, shows good form. He is leaning slightly forward, with knees bent.

Early peoples probably did not ski for recreation as many modern people do. Hunters most likely used skis to find game and to carry food back to their families. Warriors may also have used skis in winter battles.

The first sledges, or sleighs, were flat boards used to drag things over land. That technology may sound simple, but sledges mark a significant advance in people's ability to transport heavy loads. Sledges can be pulled over slick or uneven ground. They can move across both sand and snow. The addition of skilike runners at the bottom of a sledge made it easier to pull heavy loads over snow and ice. With runners, less of the vehicle's flat surface rubbed against the ground.

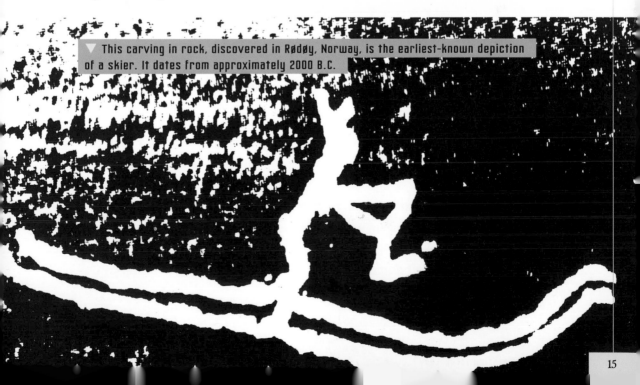

▼ This carving in rock, discovered in Rødøy, Norway, is the earliest-known depiction of a skier. It dates from approximately 2000 B.C.

Archaeologists believe that people used sledges as early as 3500 B.C. During this period, people in the Middle East kept records on clay tablets. A clay tablet found in the ancient city of Uruk, in present-day Iraq, shows carved line drawings of sledges and other transportation tools.

> **"Should a native come to the side of a river which he does not wish to swim, he supplies himself with a boat in a very expeditious manner. . . . As soon as he reaches the opposite shore, he lands, pushes the canoe back into the river, and abandons it, knowing that to make a second canoe will not be nearly so troublesome as to take care of the first."**

—John George Wood, British natural history writer, on the skill and speed of aborigine boatmakers, 1870

BEASTS OF BURDEN

The hunter-gatherer lifestyle was common until about 10,000 B.C. Then some people in the ancient Middle East began to form permanent villages and farms. They grew grain, vegetables, and fruit. They domesticated wild animals.

Domesticating is similar to taming. Domesticated animals live among humans instead of with their own wild relatives. Ancient peoples might have used trained dogs to pull travois and other vehicles. Researchers have discovered the remains of domesticated dogs, some as much as ten thousand years old, in China, Germany, and elsewhere.

People later harnessed larger animals, such as oxen and buffalo, to vehicles. With the power of these animals, people could move enormous loads over great distances. People also used asses to pull their vehicles. Asses are related to horses and donkeys. These animals once lived wild in the Mediterranean area.

Domesticated asses are slower than horses but gentler and more sure-footed. Early traders used asses as pack animals. People loaded cargo on the animals' backs for long trips. After the invention of the wheel, warriors used asses to pull chariots.

Camels were another means of transportation in ancient times. There are two kinds of camels. The dromedary, or Arabian camel, has one hump. The Bactrian camel has two. Both camels have been domesticated since ancient times. Their humps store nutrients that allow camels to live for long periods without water or food. Dromedaries have thick, wide hooves that help them move across hot desert sand. These camels can even close their nostrils to avoid inhaling dust. The Bactrian camel is more suited to rocky, cooler regions.

People riding dromedaries could cover more than 100 miles (161 km) per day. A Bactrian camel could carry up to 1,000 pounds (454 kilograms) of cargo and cover up to 30 miles (48 km) per day. Camels also supplied travelers with milk. When camels died or were killed, people ate their meat. When camels shed their long hair every summer, people wove it into fabric.

Use of the camel was a great advance in the history of land transportation. Camels allowed people to establish regular contact with other groups and to develop trade routes across vast deserts.

▲ This stone relief shows ancient people using camels to carry goods. This carving is from the ancient city of Nineveh in modern-day Iraq. It is from the eighth century B.C.

CHAPTER TWO

THE ANCIENT MIDDLE EAST

▲ Ancient peoples often settled near rivers, such as the Tigris River in present-day Iraq. Rivers offered a source of food and water and a means of transportation.

Around 6000 B.C., several distinct cultures began to develop in the ancient Middle East—the region where Asia, Africa, and Europe meet. This region contains the Fertile Crescent, an arc of land extending from the eastern Mediterranean Sea to the Persian Gulf. Because the land was good for farming, people settled there in permanent villages. Some people settled between the Tigris and Euphrates rivers in present-day Iraq, Syria, and Turkey. The Greeks later named the region Mesopotamia, which means "between rivers."

Sumer is the earliest known civilization in Mesopotamia or elsewhere. The Sumerians invented the wheel, a system of writing called cuneiform, and other technologies. The Phoenicians built great port cities such as Sidon and

Tyre. The Phoenicians established distant trading posts, including the famous city of Carthage in northern Africa. Other groups in Mesopotamia included the Babylonians and the Assyrians.

RAFTS, FLOATS, AND RIVERBOATS

Around 2000 B.C., the Assyrians built boats called *keleks*. These boats were the forerunners of modern inflatable rafts. Keleks were made from many individual sheepskins. People sewed them to form airtight bags and inflated them like balloons. They fastened the inflated skins under a frame of strong willow rods. A platform covered with reeds or moss sat atop the skins. Large keleks contained as many as twenty inflated sheepskins. Like modern rafts, keleks could bounce off rocks and zoom through strong rapids without damage. They were ideal for carrying passengers and goods safely through mountain streams.

The Assyrians also used inflated sheepskins as individual floats. Ancient wall carvings show people floating in the water on inflated skins. They probably used the floats more for work than play. It took a great deal of time and effort to prepare a sheepskin with airtight seams. The floats probably were far too expensive as toys. The carvings show men floating alongside keleks and apparently helping steer the rafts.

The Assyrians made yet another kind of boat from flat sheepskins. It was a circular riverboat for transporting cargo, soldiers, and civilians. Assyrian boatbuilders stretched the skins over a framework of willow branches or reeds. They sealed the seams between skins shut to prevent leaks. Some of the boats could hold only one or two people. Others could carry heavy cargo. Ancient writers said that the biggest boats could carry five thousand "talents." A talent is an ancient unit of weight. Five talents added up to about 57 pounds (26 kg).

THE SAIL

Most early peoples used oars and paddles to power their boats. The Phoenicians were possibly the first people to realize the advantages of wind

▼ This model of an Assyrian kelek, or raft, is based on stone carvings from the eighth century B.C. Assyrians used keleks to transport goods down the Tigris River.

> "[Assyrian riverboats] are steered by two men, who stand upright and wield a paddle each; one of them pulls the paddle towards his body, while the other pushes his paddle away from his body. These boats vary in size from very large downwards; the largest of them can manage cargo weighing five thousand talents [290,000 lbs. or 131,542 kg]."

—Herodotus, Greek historian, marveling at Assyrian riverboats after a visit to the Middle East, fifth century B.C.

power over human power. They introduced sails on their *gauli*. These round ships were used for long sea voyages, starting around 3000 B.C. Phoenician boatbuilders made sails from heavy fabric such as linen.

Gauli were the first freighters, or large cargo ships. The word *gauli* comes from a Phoenician term meaning "milk pail," which the gauli resembled. The design may have looked awkward, but the ships could carry more goods than any earlier boat. The Phoenicians also used the sturdy gauli as a warship.

Gauli relied on a single large sail fixed in one position. It could not be raised or lowered in response to changing wind conditions like a modern sail. Gauli and vessels like them could make progress only when the wind blew in the right direction. Unfavorable winds and storms often disrupted ancient sea transport.

Gauli also had oars. Sailors used them mainly to steer the ships as they entered or left harbors. In wartime, captains relied on the gauli's sail as much as possible. They conserved the strength of the rowers for battle. But just before battle, sailors removed the gauli's sail and mast and left them on a nearby beach for safekeeping. Ancient warships often rammed one another. A collision could knock the mast off one or both of the vessels.

HORSEPOWER

Ancient cave paintings and carvings on animal tusks suggest that humans have known about horses for more than thirty thousand years. Cave paintings often show people hunting horses. Early people probably regarded the animals as a food source, not as transportation.

Sometime between 4000 and 3000 B.C., people in the ancient Middle East tamed wild horses. They captured them, fed them, and tended to their illnesses and injuries. A small clay figurine found north of modern-day Damascus, Syria, depicts a domesticated horse. The figurine dates to about 2300 B.C. By this time, it would have been common to see a horse in captivity.

At first people probably kept horses for meat, milk, and goods that could be made from horsehair and horsehide. Later, people used horses to carry packs on trade routes. Some experts also think that ancient people kept horses mainly to breed mules. A mule is the offspring of a female horse and a male donkey. Mules look a lot like horses but have larger ears, smaller hooves, and tufted tails. They are more reliable than horses on unsteady ground.

SADDLE UP!

Early horses weren't very large. Most horses probably measured not more than twelve hands in height at the shoulder. (The width of a human hand—about 4 inches, or 10 centimeters—is the standard measure of horse height.) The rump was the highest part of a horse's back. A rider in the ancient Middle East had to sit on the horse's rump or his feet would drag on the ground.

Eventually early peoples began to raise horses for greater size, breeding their largest horses together. Horseback riding became more practical as horses grew larger and stronger. Experts aren't sure when horse breeding began. But riding on horseback became popular in the ancient Middle East after around 2000 B.C.

Early riders controlled their horses with a whip in one hand and a rein attached to the animal's nose ring in the other. People in Russia and eastern

This Syrian relief from Persepolis in present-day Iran shows people using small horses to transport gifts to a king. The carving dates from the fifth century B.C.

Europe invented mouth bits, bridles, and other control technology between 4000 and 3000 B.C. At first people placed simple blankets on horses' backs to protect themselves from horsehair scratches. Later, they created leather saddles.

Eventually, horses became essential in warfare. The Hittites, who occupied present-day Turkey, began riding horse-drawn chariots in battle as early as the 1700s B.C. Around the same time or soon after, the Assyrians, the Persians, and others also used horses to pull war chariots. By the ninth century B.C., cavalry warfare (with riders on horses) was more common than warfare with horse-drawn vehicles.

A soldier's life often depended on the stamina and training of his horse. Around 1350 B.C., a master horseman named Kikkuli wrote the first systematic plan for the care and feeding of the chariot horse. Kikkuli was

from Mitanni, a large state in modern-day northern Syria. Here is part of
Kikkuli's advice for keeping a horse strong and healthy:

> Day 2—Pace one league [3 miles, or 4.8 km], run one furlong
> [0.1 mile, or 0.2 km]. Feed two handsful grass, one of clover, four
> handsful barley. Graze all night.
>
> Day 4—Pace two leagues [6 miles, or 9.7 km] in morning, one
> at night. No water all day. Grass at night.
>
> Day 5—Pace two leagues, run 20 furlongs [2.4 miles, or 3.8
> km] out and 30 furlongs [3.8 miles, or 6 km] home. Put rugs
> on. After sweating, give one pail of salted water and one pail of
> malt-water. Take to river and wash down. Swim horses. Take to
> stable and give further pail of malted water and pail of salted
> water. Wash and swim again. Feed at night one bushel boiled
> barley with chaff.
>
> Day 11—Anoint all over with butter.

Why butter? Ancient people sometimes massaged their sore muscles and
joints with butter. They probably considered it a tonic for horses as well.

AROUND COMES THE WHEEL

No other technology can match the wheel in its simplicity and its impact on
society. Wheeled vehicles can move quickly and efficiently. Wheels provide
the basis for gears, pulleys, and other machines.

The oldest known depiction of a wheel appears on a clay tablet from about
3500 B.C. It is the same Mesopotamian tablet on which a picture of an ancient
sledge appears. The tablet shows a sledge with two small disks attached.
Researchers believe the vehicle is actually a four-wheeled cart.

People did not invent the first wheel for transportation. Archaeologists think
the first wheels were potter's wheels. These wooden disks spun horizontally.

THE FIRST MAPS

Where is it? How do I get there? What is the fastest route? People have asked such questions for thousands of years.

Early peoples probably made the first maps by scratching in the soil with sticks. Perhaps they drew the location of rivers, lakes, mountains, and herds of game. Archaeologists suspect that some cave paintings and etchings found on animal tusks may be early maps. But the pictures may also just be decorative illustrations.

Clay tablets from Mesopotamia with all the essential characteristics of maps date to around 2300 B.C. These tablets have diagrams of land features and clearly visible markers for the cardinal points—north, south, east, and west. Many early Mesopotamian maps appear to be legal records of land purchases. They mark off the exact dimensions of lots and fields. Other maps were probably used to help transport people and goods over long distances.

One ancient Babylonian map, possibly the earliest world map, shows Earth as it was known to the Babylonians around 500 B.C. The Babylonians had little knowledge of what lay beyond their own territory. The map depicts the world as a disk, with the Persian Gulf, Babylon, and other Middle Eastern countries in the center. The mapmaker showed an immense ocean surrounding these countries. Beyond the ocean were four remote regions believed to be at the very edge of the world.

◄ This cuneiform map from Babylon dates from the 600s B.C. The map shows the world known to Babylonians, with their country as the center.

People used them to shape lumps of clay into vessels. Experts are not certain when or how the potter's wheel became a cart wheel. Perhaps carpenters moved newly completed potter's wheels by rolling them. Perhaps children rolled the wheels as toys. Then someone attached them to axles (a rod around which the wheel turns) made of a stick and put a sledge on top.

The wheel was most likely invented only once, in Mesopotamia. It then quickly spread to other civilizations. In Europe researchers have found the remains of four-wheeled, animal-drawn wagons that may be as much as five thousand years old. Archaeologists have also found evidence of wheel use in India just after 3500 B.C. and in Egypt by 2500 B.C.

Some cultures tried the wheel and found it unsuitable. People in parts of Asia and the Middle East preferred camels to wheeled carts. Camels were more efficient for travel over desert sands and rough terrain.

BETTER WHEELS AND AXLES

At first, wheel making probably involved little more than cutting a slab of wood from a round tree trunk. People later realized that sturdier wheels could be made from combining several separate pieces of wood. For roughly one thousand years after their invention, wheels were made from three thick pieces of wood, bound by strips of wood fastened around the outside.

People eventually learned to reduce the weight of the three-part wheel by carving out inner sections of the disk. Inventors in Mesopotamia developed the spoked wheel around 2000 B.C. Spokes are thin bars connecting a wheel's rim and hub. Spoked wheels were much lighter than solid wheels and moved faster. The use of spokes quickly spread beyond the Middle East.

By 1400 B.C., Egyptian woodworkers were making strong, light wheels by putting together separate rims, spokes, and hubs. Woodworkers joined the parts and adjusted them for proper balance. They nailed strips of copper or

This relief, found in modern-day Turkey, shows a chariot with a spoked wheel. The sculpture dates from 1500–1100 B.C. Spoked wheels are lighter than solid wheels and allow vehicles to move faster.

bronze to the outside of the wheels to reduce wear. These strips were the first tires. The Egyptians first used these improved wheels on expensive racing and war chariots.

An axle that connected wheel to vehicle was essential. The first axles were strong wooden poles that extended through a central hole in the wheel. A peg through the axle kept the wheel attached. Some axles were fixed to and turned with wheels. Other axles allowed wheels to roll independently.

CHAPTER THREE

ANCIENT EGYPT

Around 8000 B.C., northern Africa's wet climate became drier. Hunter-gatherers in the area began to move east, toward the Nile River in Egypt. The Nile flows for 4,145 miles (6,671 km), making it the longest river in the world.

By about 7000 B.C., people had built farming settlements along the river. The Nile flooded its banks every July. The floodwater soaked the soil and deposited fertile, mudlike silt on the surrounding land. Early Egyptian farmers grew an abundance of wheat, barley, vegetables, and fruits.

▼ The Nile River has been the center of culture in northern Africa since around 8000 B.C.

The Nile was a natural pathway for transporting goods and people. Traders in reed ships floated with the current. They deposited their cargoes at Egyptian cities such as Thebes, Memphis, and Giza. Then they sailed and rowed against the current back to home ports. From the mouth of the Nile, Egyptian merchants established trading routes that led to Asia, Greece, and other places.

NAVIGATING THE NILE

The first Egyptian boats were rafts made from tightly woven papyrus reeds. Boaters used poles to guide the rafts through shallow water. A wall painting completed around 3500 B.C. shows crews of rowers in papyrus boats. One crew member uses a steering paddle to guide each boat.

Egyptian boat makers eventually attached a mast and square sail to their vessels. The sail was not stuck in a fixed position as it was on Phoenician ships. Instead, the sail could be raised or lowered as needed. Ships traveling south on the Nile, against the current, required a sail. Luckily for the sailors, prevailing winds in Egypt blow in from the north. When traveling north, sailors lowered the sail and ran with the current. The ships also had oars for power in calm weather and for maneuvering near docks. Passengers, crew, and cargo rode on deck under cloth shelters. Some Egyptian ships also had cabins beneath the deck for passengers, with shades that rolled up and down.

This stone relief from the tomb of Egyptian official Ptahhotep (late 2500s to early 2400s B.C.) shows ancient Egyptians riding on a papyrus raft.

SEAFARING VESSELS

The Egyptians built larger boats to navigate trade routes on the
Mediterranean Sea. Some of these vessels were 180 feet (55 m) long and
60 feet (18 m) wide. In 1954 an Egyptian archaeologist found the remains
of a magnificent ship buried in a sandpit, under heavy stone slabs, near
the Great Pyramid of Giza. The Great Pyramid is the tomb of Khufu, an
Egyptian pharaoh (king) who lived around 2600 B.C. It is the largest of several
pyramids on the outskirts of Cairo, Egypt.

▼ Experts reassembled this Egyptian barge from well-preserved
segments found near the tomb of Egyptian king Khufu. The boat dates
from around 2600 B.C.

▲ Egyptian workers built the pyramid tombs of kings Menkaure, Khafre, and Khufu *(from left to right)* more than four thousand years ago. Archaeologists marvel at the ancient Egyptians' ability to move the huge stones required for the projects. Workers used sledges to pull large stones away from quarries. They used rafts to float the stones along the Nile to construction sites.

The ship found near Khufu's pyramid was buried in 1,224 separate pieces. Experts spent more than a decade carefully putting the ship back together. The reconstructed vessel was more than 143 feet (44 m) long. Possibly no one ever actually sailed on the ship. The vessel contained oars but was not watertight. Researchers believe the ship was strictly a ceremonial barge.

Ancient Egyptians believed in life after death. To ensure a person's well-being in the afterlife, Egyptians carefully preserved the person's body. They also buried him or her with items that would reflect his or her mortal life. Khufu's barge was most likely meant to assist him on his spiritual journey.

Archaeologists have found model boats in the tombs of other Egyptian leaders. Some of the boats are equipped with canopies, sails, and even model rowers. Like Khufu's ship, these boats may never have actually floated.

EGYPTIAN MAPS

Ancient Egyptians carved maps in stone, drew maps on papyrus scrolls, and painted maps on pottery and tomb walls. With a single known exception, however, these maps were not intended to help people find their way from one location to another. Instead, the maps were religious and symbolic documents. Some showed secret routes to the afterlife. Others illustrated astronomers' concepts of the universe, including the realms of Egyptian gods and goddesses.

▲ The Turin Papyrus, created around 1200 B.C., is the only known usable (not symbolic) ancient Egyptian map. The map shows the route to gold mines in a mountainous region of Egypt along the Red Sea.

THE ANCIENT SUEZ CANAL

The Suez Canal, a modern Egyptian waterway, gives ships a shortcut from the Mediterranean Sea to the Red Sea. Without this 101-mile (162 km) channel, freighters, oil tankers, passenger ships, and warships traveling east from Europe would have to sail around the tip of Africa to reach ports in the Indian Ocean. The canal reduces transportation times between Europe and Asia by weeks. It reduces distances traveled by thousands of miles.

Many historians trace the canal's origins to a French diplomat named Ferdinand-Marie de Lesseps. In 1854 de Lesseps enlisted the Egyptian government in the canal construction project. But another Suez Canal was built more than three thousand years earlier. In the thirteenth century B.C., ancient Egyptian engineers dug a canal that also allowed ships to pass directly from the Mediterranean Sea to the Red Sea. It followed a different route than the modern Suez Canal. It linked a branch of the Nile River north of Cairo with the Red Sea. Historians believe the project originated either with Seti I, a pharaoh who reigned from about 1290 to 1279 B.C., or with Ramesses II, who ruled from 1279 to 1213 B.C.

The early canal gradually declined in usefulness. It was filled in by blowing sand and forgotten. But several centuries later, other Egyptian leaders recognized the benefits of a passage between the Nile and the Red Sea. Many historians believe that construction of a new canal began under Necho II, who ruled Egypt from 610 to 595 B.C. The project stalled following Necho's death.

Later, King Darius I of Persia, who lived from 550 to 486 B.C., ruled Egypt. He also ordered the building of a waterway to the Red Sea. Unlike the rulers before him, he saw the canal completed in his lifetime. Darius was very proud

▲ This aerial image of the Suez Canal in Egypt was taken from the International Space Station in 2006. Modern engineers were not the first to create a canal from the Mediterranean Sea to the Red Sea.

"I ordered that this canal be dug from the river which is called Nile, which flows in Egypt, to the sea which goes from Persia. Then the canal was dug as I commanded, and ships sailed from Egypt through this canal to Persia, according to my will."

—Persian king Darius I, from a pillar celebrating the canal's construction, fifth century B.C.

of the achievement. He boasted about it through carved messages on granite pillars along the waterway.

Darius's engineers may have been aware of the earlier waterway connecting the Mediterranean Sea and the Red Sea. Some visible remains of the first Suez Canal must still have existed during Darius's reign. Some archaeologists think the engineers may have saved unnecessary labor by repairing segments of the earlier canal whenever possible.

SLEDGES AND PAVED ROADS

Some of the stones used to build Egypt's pyramids, sculptures, and other monuments weigh more than 4,000 pounds (1,814 kg). Archaeologists believe sledges played a big role in moving these heavy blocks. Gangs of men transported stones on sledges from rock quarries to the Nile and onto barges and from the barges to building sites. Workers also used sledges to move stones up temporary earthen ramps and into position at pyramids.

▲ This three-thousand-year-old Egyptian papyrus shows workers dragging building blocks on a sledge.

People seldom develop new technology unless a need exists. Sometimes one form of technology creates the need for another. Archaeologists believe that such a link exists between sledges and paved roads. Sledges were not always an effective way to carry blocks of stone across the desert. Occasionally, heavy loads sank into the sand. So the Egyptians decided to pave the sand.

The remains of one paved road extend about 7.5 miles (12 km) through the desert southwest of Cairo. Discovered by the U.S. Geological Survey in 1994, the path is thought to be the oldest paved road in the world. Artifacts (remains of a human culture) found along the road date between 2600 and 2134 B.C. The road had an average width of 6.5 feet (2 m) and was made from slabs of sandstone and limestone laid end to end.

Ancient Egyptians built the road to haul stones on sledges from a rock quarry to a dock at ancient Lake Moeris near the Nile River. A natural canal connected the lake to the Nile. At the dock of the lake, workers loaded stones onto barges and floated down the channel to the Nile. The barges then floated downriver to pyramid sites.

▼ An ancient paved road leads to the Pyramid of Menkaure at Giza. Paved roads developed as an easier means of moving heavy loads across sandy terrain.

CHAPTER FOUR

ANCIENT INDIA

People in western India began settling into villages around 4000 B.C. Within one thousand years, one of the world's greatest civilizations had emerged in this region. It covered an area of around 300,000 square miles (777,000 sq. km) in modern-day Pakistan and India. It is called the Indus Valley Civilization because it developed along the Indus River.

About 1700 B.C., people began to leave the Indus Valley. Experts believe that floods or changing river patterns may have caused the end of the Indus Valley Civilization. Two hundred years later, Aryans, a warlike people from central Asia, invaded India. They drove the earlier inhabitants southward.

Aryan invaders spread throughout northern India and settled into villages. Around 518 B.C., warriors from Persia took control of northwestern India, including parts of modern-day Pakistan. Around 324 B.C., a new empire took form. Chandragupta Maurya, a ruler descended from India's central Asian conquerors, united all northern India. The Mauryan Empire controlled the north for about one hundred years. It dissolved after the death of Chandragupta's grandson Ashoka. But another empire, the Gupta Empire, took the place of the Mauryans. Throughout these many changes, people from central Asia continued coming to India.

ROAD TRAVEL

In the fifth century B.C., King Darius I of Persia oversaw the development of an extensive system of roadways. The system included the Royal Road.

The Royal Road was an east-west route that began in the Persian capital of Susa (in present-day Iran) and ran to northern India. The road was more than 1,700 miles (2,736 km) long.

Regional governments helped merchants and other travelers by building rest houses along the Royal Road. These houses functioned much like modern

▼ The Indus River flows through present-day Pakistan and India. Land near the river formed the center of the Indus Valley Civilization until about 1700 B.C.

▲ This pillar, featuring advice from Emperor Ashoka, has stood since the third century B.C. In modern times, it stands in Vaishali, Bihar, India.

motels. People at the houses provided travelers with information about the location of additional rest houses and other landmarks. Soldiers stationed along the Royal Road kept a look out for lawbreakers, much like modern state troopers or highway patrol officers do.

Ancient India also had the equivalent of transportation officials. Indian rulers had officials in different regions oversee maintenance on the Royal Road. The officials made sure that the road was free of large rocks or fallen trees. They also saw that road markers were correctly positioned so that travelers could keep track of distances.

Emperor Ashoka, who ruled from about 269 to 232 B.C., ordered that stone signs be posted along many roads in northern India. These huge pillars weighed up to 50 tons (45 metric tons). Workers hauled the pillars to their roadside sites on oxcarts. The pillars were inscribed with Ashoka's words of wisdom and advice for daily living.

"It is good to give, but there is no gift, no service, like the gift of righteousness."

—Emperor Ashoka, from a roadside pillar inscribed with his advice, third century B.C.

GREAT TRADERS

The Indus River valley was very fertile. Farmers in the region constructed dams and canals to control the flow of the river and to irrigate (supply with water) land farther away. The farmers produced more than enough crops to supply the population. Ancient Indian farmers could trade surplus crops for metals, timber, dye, and other products. These farmers were the first to grow cotton. It too became a valuable item for trade.

Indian merchants exported fine cloth, jewels, pepper, and other spices along the famous Silk Road. This trade route extended from China to the Mediterranean Sea. The Roman port of Ostia, 16 miles (26 km) from Rome, had warehouses laden with pepper and other Indian goods. The Indians traded extensively for gold. In fact, Roman merchants traded so much gold to Indians that the Roman emperor Nero banned the import of Indian peppercorns to prevent more gold from leaving Rome.

ELEPHANT POWER

For travel, trade, warfare, and construction work, the ancient Indians used the world's biggest and most powerful beast of burden—the elephant. Male Indian elephants grow to between 9 and 10 feet (2.7 to 3 m) in height and can weigh up to 8,000

▼ This terra-cotta figure of an elephant came from a tomb in modern-day Turkey. It dates from around 200 B.C. The peoples of ancient India began to ride elephants at least a century earlier, by the 300s B.C.

pounds (3,600 kg). A fully grown female Indian elephant stands about 1 foot (0.3 m) shorter and weighs several hundred pounds less. Although male elephants are more powerful than females, workers used female elephants more often for transportation because they were easier to control.

Ancient Indians knew that elephants were intelligent and could be trained to perform certain tasks. They captured calves (young elephants) in the wild and assigned each calf a keeper. An elephant's keeper stayed with the animal for life.

Elephants transported rulers and other wealthy people on saddles or in small covered compartments. They also carried merchandise along trade routes. Elephants were ideal for logging in jungles because of their massive size. They could smash their way through heavy undergrowth while carrying logs with their powerful trunks. Some modern logging operations in India still use elephants.

Ancient Indians also used elephants in warfare. Soldiers rode on saddles fastened around the animals' necks. Soldiers controlled their elephants with voice commands and by hitting them with long sticks. In wartime, elephants even wore heavy leather armor for protection.

▼ Logging companies in modern India still use elephants to harvest and transport logs from otherwise unreachable parts of jungles.

ANCIENT INDIAN BOATING

The people of ancient India used a wide variety of seacraft. The landscape along India's coast changes from region to region. So did the designs of ancient Indian boats. On the central west coast, people used boats such as dugout canoes. Later, outriggers were common. These ships have beams extending from the side to support the ship's mast.

People on India's east coast also used dugout canoes. People used *masula*, boats with planks and frames bound together by stiff rope. Masula were typically used for fishing and travel to nearby areas. Ancient peoples sailed along east India's northern coast in boats built with flat planks. These boats could be conveniently docked on the calm northeastern banks.

Plank boats could not dock as easily upon east India's southern coastline because of the area's harsh breaking waves. Log rafts called catamarans were more practical for sailing in the southeast. Travelers in catamarans could safely cross the dangerous surf and then take their boats apart to dry on sandy shores. Archaeologists believe a fishing community in the modern Indian state of Tamil Nadu developed the catamaran sometime before A.D. 500.

Scholars are not sure when the ancient Indians first began to use elephants for combat. A battle between the forces of Macedonian warrior Alexander the Great and King Porus of Paurava (a kingdom in the Punjab region of India and Pakistan) marks one of the earliest recorded instances of elephant warfare. Alexander encountered two hundred of these fighting animals when he and his army of 120,000 soldiers invaded Paurava in 326 B.C.

THE BIG-TOE STIRRUP

Ancient Indians also fought on horseback. Indian riders introduced a major advance in warfare and transportation with the development of a simple device, the stirrup. A stirrup is a support for a rider's foot that hangs down from each side of a saddle.

Archaeologists have examined depictions of horses on ancient statues, coins, and other artifacts. These artifacts show that for thousands of years, most early peoples did not use stirrups. Evidence suggests that ancient Indian riders introduced the first verified stirrups between 300 and 200 B.C.

The stirrup is so simple that some people might not even regard it as technology. But the stirrup was a revolutionary tool. Stirrups made horses more accessible. Without stirrups, riders had to vault onto horses, and only people in top physical condition could jump so high.

▼ This relief from India shows a man on horseback with stirrups. The relief is from the second century B.C. Stirrups made it much easier for riders to mount horses.

The ancient Indian stirrup consisted of a fiber or leather thong. A rider attached the thong to a saddle and draped it against the horse's side. At the bottom was a loop, just big enough for the rider's big toe. Why the big toe rather than the entire foot? If you have the answer, archaeologists would love to know. In fact, the big-toe design may have slowed adoption of the stirrup by other groups. A stirrup of this kind could be used only in warm places where people went barefoot.

With stirrups, warriors were more balanced on their horses and could fight more effectively. This silver coin from Pakistan showing a king on horseback dates from the first century B.C.

Stirrups transformed the horse into a better war machine. The saddle gave riders improved balance from front to back, and stirrups added side-to-side balance. With a stirrup and a saddle, the horse and rider became a single stable unit. With his weight on the stirrups, a rider could carry a long lance or a spear, brace it firmly against his body, and charge an enemy. He could lift a heavy sword or battle-ax high above his head and slash down hard without losing his balance.

Merchants who traveled the Silk Road carried stirrup technology from India to China and eventually from India to Europe. King Charles Martel, who ruled the area that eventually became Germany and Belgium, adopted the stirrup in the eighth century A.D. Stirrups gave Charles's soldiers an advantage in warfare.

CHAPTER FIVE

ANCIENT CHINA

Chinese society emerged between 5000 and 3000 B.C. in the Yellow River valley of northern China. There, early peoples settled into small farming villages. The river provided water for drinking, irrigation, fishing, and transportation. When the river flooded the land, it left behind layers of rich soil for farming.

China has many waterways, but few are connected to one another naturally. So the ancient Chinese developed technology to suit their geography. They dug numerous canals. They created a watery transportation network that linked rivers from many parts of China.

▼ The Yellow River was the backbone of early Chinese society. As the society expanded, the Chinese dug canals to link different parts of China by water.

AMAZING CANAL BUILDERS

Eastern China is home to the world's largest canal, the Grand Canal. The Grand Canal covers nearly 1,120 miles (1,800 km) north to south. It provides passage between the modern Chinese cities of Beijing and Hangzhou. The construction of the Grand Canal began around 486 B.C. Work on the canal continued for more than one hundred years.

In one sense, construction of the Grand Canal started even earlier. A smaller canal, the Hong Gou (Canal of Flying Geese), already linked China's Yellow River to several other rivers throughout the country. The northernmost part of the Grand Canal later incorporated a section of the Hong Gou. Researchers are unsure when the Hong Gou was first constructed. It may have existed in some form as early as the sixth century B.C.

Until 221 B.C., China was made up of warring states. Emperor Shih-huang-ti unified these states to form a single powerful nation. During his reign (221–210 B.C.), Shih-huang-ti ordered the construction of another canal: the Lingqu, or Magic Canal. This 23-mile (37 km) canal crossed mountainous terrain in southern China. It connected the Xiang and Li rivers. Archaeologists think the Magic Canal was the first canal to connect rivers across a watershed (an area in which all water throughout or underneath the land drains into the same body of water).

This illustration depicts a dragon boat moving down the Grand Canal in China in the A.D. 600s.

THE MARVELOUS JUNK

The ancient Chinese sailed down canals in a ship that came to be known as a junk. Junks were boxy and ungainly. They had a flat bottom, a high stern (rear), and a low bow (front).

The junk lacked components that most modern people regard as fundamental to ships. It had no keel (a long beam along the bottom of a boat) and no sternpost (an upright post at a ship's stern). On most boats, keels act like a backbone and help hold everything together. Sternposts help support other parts of a boat's back end. Even without these parts, junks were among the strongest and most seaworthy vessels ever designed.

The junk's high stern allowed the deck to stay dry when waves crashed from behind. The design also assured that the ship would safely turn with its bow to the wind when anchored. Its flat bottom allowed safe sailing through shallow water and easy beaching onshore.

▼ Boxy ships called junks can still be seen traveling China's waterways.

A rudder, or heavy steering oar, compensated for the lack of a keel. The rudder was mounted in a watertight space. It extended through the boat's deck and hull (main body). The rudder could be raised in shallow water to prevent damage and lowered again with ease. Sails were made of bamboo mats or linen fabric. Crew members could open and close them quickly with changing wind conditions.

A major advantage of the junk's boxy design was the exceptionally strong hull. Bulkheads—solid walls made from heavy wooden planks—ran lengthwise and crosswise inside the hull. They divided the hull into twelve or more watertight compartments. Bulkheads acted as barriers to incoming seawater. The compartments limited flooding if the ship struck rock or was damaged in battle. A hole in the hull might flood one compartment, but it probably would not sink the entire ship.

HOW THE JUNK GOT ITS NAME

The name *junk* has nothing to do with garbage or poor quality. People from the Southeast Asian island of Java used the term *jong* to refer to all sailing vessels. This included the bulky Chinese ships that sometimes visited Java's shores.

In the 1600s, Portuguese and Dutch travelers began visiting Java. These travelers began using the Javanese term for boat. But the European sailors pronounced it "junco." English speakers adopted the word *junk* as a term for Chinese ships after hearing the Portuguese and the Dutch use similar terms.

> ## "[There are] all manner of odd-looking craft, but none so odd as the Chinese junk. The junk . . . looks as if it were copied from some picture on an old teacup."

—Nathaniel Hawthorne, U.S. writer, remarking on Chinese ships seen during a visit to Britain, 1853

THE WOODEN OX

The ancient Chinese also made innovations in land transportation. Chinese inventors devised a simple yet ingenious tool for moving heavy loads. Their device consisted of a wooden frame, a single wheel, and two handles. We know it as the wheelbarrow.

With the wheelbarrow, one person could carry a load that had previously required two or three people. One soldier with a wheelbarrow could carry enough food to supply four others for up to three months. Ancient Chinese wheelbarrows had one wheel in the middle of a cart, directly under the load. With this arrangement, the pusher's main work involved balancing and steering. (Wheelbarrows with a wheel at one end require much more effort to lift and support a load.)

Some sources credit Chinese general Zhuge Liang with inventing the wheelbarrow around A.D. 230. Zhuge recognized that the wheelbarrow was a simple, inexpensive means of transporting large quantities of food and weapons during wartime. Records from about the fifth century A.D. mention his detailed plans for a "wooden ox" and "gliding horse." Experts are not sure of the difference between Zhuge's "ox" and "horse," but many believe that he intended the ox to be pulled from the front and the horse to be pushed from behind.

Historians do not doubt that Zhuge Liang helped make the wheelbarrow more popular or perhaps improved on earlier designs. But evidence from

◄ This Chinese brick carving from the first century A.D. shows a man pushing an early wheelbarrow. Wheelbarrows made it possible for a single person to move heavy loads.

▼ Later Chinese wheelbarrows placed the wheel underneath the load, such as in this model, rather than in front. The new position required less effort to lift the wheelbarrow.

stone carvings dating from before Zhuge's lifetime confirms that he was not the first person to develop such a craft. In fact, the wheelbarrow was probably in use by 206 B.C. Outside of battle, the Chinese used wheelbarrows to transport people and goods such as rice and vegetables. Some later versions of wheelbarrows could hold several passengers.

THE SILK ROAD

The Han dynasty (family of rulers) led China from 206 B.C. to A.D. 200. China underwent great economic growth during this period. Chinese merchants drove groups of camels from cities along the Yellow River through central Asia to the Middle East. These merchants traded jade and bronze for rugs, horses, glass, and other products. But the main Chinese export was silk, a soft, shimmery fabric. So much silk traveled over the China-to-Middle-East route that it became known as the Silk Road.

▲ A man and a Bactrian camel travel along the Silk Road in modern-day northwestern China. The Silk Road was once a major trade route, connecting mainland China to the Mediterranean region.

Few merchants made the entire trip. The Silk Road extended thousands of miles overland from Ch'ang-an in east central China through modern Siberia to the eastern coast of the Mediterranean. Traders continued by sea to Rome and Venice. Goods typically changed hands many times along the road.

The Silk Road came to serve as an ancient technological superhighway. Merchants exchanged information about new ideas and innovations. For instance, the tandem hitching of horses (one behind the other) saved space on narrow roads. The Chinese began this practice and passed it on to people in the Middle East and Europe.

A SPOON POINTS THE WAY

In *The Book of the Devil Valley Master*, written in the fourth century B.C., Chinese philosopher Su Ch'in states: "When the people of Cheng go out to collect jade, they carry a south-pointer with them, so as not to lose their way." The "south-pointer," or "magic spoon," Su Ch'in refers to is the magnetic compass. Wang Ch'ung, another philosopher, wrote some of the other earliest-known remarks about the compass. "When the south-controlling spoon is thrown upon the ground, it comes to rest pointing at the south," Ch'ung observed.

Sailors, hikers, airplane pilots, and other travelers frequently use magnetic compasses for navigation. Compasses indicate direction with a needle that points toward Earth's north magnetic pole. With north established, people can determine other directions.

The ancient Chinese used a compass made of lodestone, a kind of iron. Craftspeople fashioned the lodestone into the shape of a ladle. When placed on a polished slab of magnetic stone, the bowl of the spoon pointed north and the handle pointed south. Marks indicating direction—north, south, east, and west—were carved on the slab's surface.

The ladle shape of ancient Chinese compasses represented the Big Dipper. This is a constellation, or group of stars, that look something like a ladle. The Big Dipper points to the North Star, which always appears to be above the North Pole.

▼ This Chinese *sinan*, or compass, consists of a lodestone ladle on a magnetic stone. It was made more than two thousand years ago.

CHAPTER SIX

THE ANCIENT AMERICAS

About thirty thousand years ago, northeastern Asia and northwestern North America were connected by a land bridge. Early peoples from Asia walked over this bridge and into North America. In modern times, the bridge is covered by a body of water called the Bering Strait. Other Asian peoples may have reached North America by walking over thick ice in the Bering Strait. Still others may have reached the Americas by boat over open stretches of ocean.

Like other ancient peoples, the first North Americans were hunters and gatherers. They probably crossed the land bridge to follow herds of bison, mastodons, and mammoths that migrated to Alaska. People then moved south through present-day Canada, onto the American Great Plains (the land west of the Mississippi River and east of the Rocky Mountains), and into present-day Mexico and Central America. These Paleo-Indians (ancient Native Americans) had reached the tip of South America by about 11,000 B.C. Different groups encountered different environmental conditions as they migrated south. Separate cultures developed throughout the Americas.

ANCIENT NORTH AMERICA

Few artifacts and no written records of the Paleo-Indians' transportation technology exist. Archaeologists assume that hunter-gatherers in North America relied on foot coverings, yokes, and other technology like that used by hunter-gatherers in Asia and elsewhere. We know for certain that Native Americans across the Great Plains relied on the travois.

▲ Native Americans on the Great Plains used the travois into the twentieth century. The travois is a simple device that allows people to move cargo more easily. This image of Plains Indians was taken in the 1900s.

The travois was a great help to peoples dealing with the Great Plains' varied landscapes and sometimes harsh weather. A traveler could pull cargo over snow or soil and through prairies or forests. Native American tribes such as the Cheyenne and the Lakota used it through the nineteenth century A.D.

For hundreds, perhaps thousands, of years, the early peoples of North America harnessed the travois to domesticated dogs. In the 1500s, Spanish explorers began to arrive in the Americas. The Spanish brought with them a more powerful load-bearing animal: the horse. Native Americans in the Great Plains soon began harnessing travois to horses as well. Peoples throughout North America also quickly adopted the practice of riding on horseback. Riding horses allowed Native Americans to be more effective in both hunting and combat.

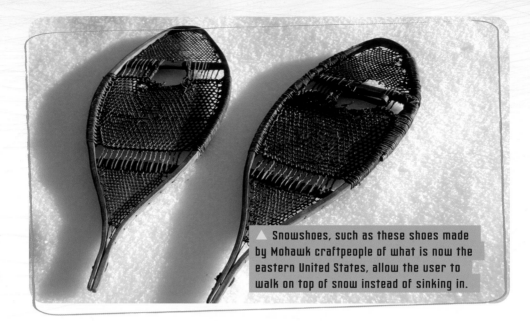

▲ Snowshoes, such as these shoes made by Mohawk craftpeople of what is now the eastern United States, allow the user to walk on top of snow instead of sinking in.

The Assiniboine and other Native American groups that lived in snowy regions used snowshoes to move quickly during hunts or long walks. Early snowshoes typically had a wooden frame with lacings made from animal hide. They kept hunters' feet from sinking into the cold, wet ground.

CANOES AND MORE

Native Americans used canoes to travel across North America's rivers and lakes. Different varieties of canoes were popular in different regions. Many peoples east of the Great Plains relied on lightweight bark canoes. Groups in southeastern North America traveled by dugout canoe as well. Dugout canoes were also common on the West Coast. Peoples in the Pacific Northwest created huge dugout boats from cedar and redwood trees. Some of these canoes measured more than 60 feet (18 m) in length.

In certain areas, Native Americans used animal skins as a boatbuilding material. Animal skin kept water from leaking into the boat, and it was a more flexible building material than wood. Peoples of the Great Plains created small "bull boats" by stretching buffalo skin over rounded wooden frames. The Inuit, who live in modern-day northern Canada, built similar boats with sealskin and walrus skin.

"Two sticks . . . are tied together so as to form a round hoop of the size you wish the canoe [to be], or as large as the skin will cover, two of those hoops are made, one for the top or brim and the [other] for the bottom, the [depth] you wish the canoe, then sticks of the same size are crossed at right angles and fastened with a throng to each hoop and also where each stick crosses the other."

—William Clark, North American explorer, on the making of a bull boat, early 1800s

◀ This Inuit canoe from the Arctic region of northeastern Canada is made of animal skin.

▼ Many eastern woodland tribes crafted birchbark canoes like this one.

MESOAMERICA

Many societies emerged in the region extending from present-day Mexico to the Isthmus of Panama in present-day Central America. Historians use the term *Mesoamerica* to describe this area and its cultures prior to the arrival of European explorers and settlers in the 1500s. Researchers have found few written records from Mesoamerica. Much of what we know about Mesoamerican transportation technology actually comes from the Spanish, who arrived in 1519.

The Olmec people lived in southern parts of Mexico between 1200 and 400 B.C. Among the Olmecs' best-known achievements is the carving and moving of huge stone heads. The heads are cube-shaped, with smooth, rounded corners and flat faces in front. They were most likely designed to honor Olmec rulers. Some of these heads stand as tall as 9 feet (2.7 m) and weigh up to 36,000 pounds (16,300 kg). Explorers and others have found seventeen stone heads, most of them at a site called San Lorenzo in southern Mexico.

▼ The Olmec people lived in present-day southern Mexico more than three thousand years ago. They carved giant heads out of a volcanic rock called basalt.

Olmec sculptors carved the heads out of a volcanic rock called basalt. This rock comes from mountains more than 40 miles (64 km) away from San Lorenzo. Researchers are not sure how the Olmec managed to move such heavy objects. It's possible that the Olmec relied on sledges, as did other ancient peoples. If so, large groups of workers probably pulled the sledges over several months.

THE AMAZING MAYA

The Maya emerged around 2500 B.C. They developed a powerful empire in modern-day southern Mexico, Guatemala, Belize, El Salvador, and Honduras. Many aspects of Mayan civilization rivaled or surpassed those of ancient Egypt and Greece. The Maya built cities with paved streets. They developed a written language and made accurate observations about the movement of the sun, the moon, the stars, and the planets. The Maya are also the first known culture to understand the mathematical concept of zero. Mayan civilization peaked between A.D. 300 and 700 and then mysteriously declined.

The Maya traded extensively throughout their area. Archaeologists have found products from the Mayan Empire's tropical lowlands in the remains of ancient settlements throughout the highlands. These products include salt, cacao (chocolate), cotton, feathers, spices, and jaguar pelts. Highland

▼ Ancient Mayan cities—such as Tikal in Guatemala—consisted of huge temples, paved streets, meeting places, and homes.

products such as jade and obsidian (a volcanic glass) have been found in the lowlands. Traders carried the products from one region to another.

The remains of Mayan ports, including one on the island of Cerritos off the northern coast of the Yucatán Peninsula in Mexico, have given archaeologists clues about Mayan sea travel. The port facilities, used between 300 B.C. and A.D. 300, included piers, docks, and an artificial canal. A seawall, more than 1,000 feet (305 m) long, protected boats in the harbor. Mayan merchants probably brought canoes full of salt, fish, and other goods to the port for trading. But despite what archaeologists know, many questions remain about Mayan transportation. Archaeologists don't know how the Maya transported food from farms to large urban areas or what vehicles they used.

UNUSUAL TRANSPORTATION HABITS

The Mesoamericans stand out among ancient cultures for the means of transportation they did not use. For example, Mesoamericans never harnessed beasts of burden. Although cultures such as the Maya may have domesticated deer for use as a food source, they did not use them as draft animals.

Nor did Mesoamericans rely on the wheel for transportation. Mesoamerican groups had plenty of wood that could have been used to make wheels. Archaeologists know that some Mesoamericans knew how to construct wheels, because they have found clay toys with wheels and axles in ancient Mayan ruins. But much of the terrain in present-day Mexico and elsewhere wasn't suitable for full-scale wheeled vehicles. Many Mesoamerican settlements were located in rugged upland regions and in tropical rain forests. Without land that was relatively flat, dry, and firm, wheeled crafts were not practical for trade or warfare.

BRIDGES OF THE INCA

The Inca lived throughout much of South America in the 1400s and 1500s. The Inca Empire included parts of present-day Colombia, Ecuador, Peru, Chile, Bolivia, and Argentina. A vast network of roads and bridges extended throughout the Inca's massive territory. In certain places, Inca bridges spanned vast river gorges. Some of these bridges were 150 feet (46 m) long or longer.

Inca builders began constructing a bridge by weaving long ropes out of plant fibers. Then they braided many ropes together to make thick cables. Five cables formed the framework of the bridge. Two of these cables were handrails. Three other cables served as the bridge floor. Bridge builders attached the five cables to stone supports on both sides of the gorge.

Builders attached pieces of wood to shorter floor cables to create a solid surface for walking. In some cases, they tied wood and branches to side cables to create walls. Inca bridges were sturdy but flexible. They swayed in the fierce winds that blew through river gorges, but they supported the weight of the people and animals that moved across them.

▼ Inca bridges, such as this one in modern-day Peru, allowed the Inca to cross gorges. The bridges were made of braided rope.

CHAPTER SEVEN

ANCIENT GREECE

Greece, birthplace of great ancient philosophers, writers, and artists, is a rugged land along the Mediterranean Sea. Ancient Greek farmers grew grapes, olives, and other fruits. But their farms were small. The Greeks had to look beyond their borders for a greater supply of food. Almost everywhere they looked, they saw ocean.

For this reason, the ancient Greeks excelled at shipbuilding, mapmaking, seafaring, trading, and naval warfare. Geography often plays a role in the development of technology. The ancient Greeks' most important contributions to transportation technology involved the sea.

In 338 B.C., Philip of Macedonia conquered the Greek city-states and established Greece as a military power. Philip's son, Alexander the Great, then conquered much of the Mediterranean and Middle Eastern world—from Egypt to western India. Greece's military strength stemmed largely part from its superior seafaring technology.

BEACONS FOR MARINERS

Lighthouses are beacons that guide sailors into harbors and warn of rocky shorelines that could sink a ship. Historians are unsure who constructed the first lighthouse. But it might have been the ancient Greeks. Some sources say that Lesches, a legendary Greek poet, described a lighthouse as early as 660 B.C. But Lesches' works were lost and are unavailable to modern-day readers.

The most famous ancient lighthouse was the Pharos of Alexandria. It was built on a rocky island (also named Pharos) off the northern coast of Egypt in the Mediterranean Sea. The Pharos stood near the great ancient city of

Alexandria. Alexander the Great founded this city in 332 B.C. It became a cultural center for the ancient Greeks.

Ptolemy II governed Egypt from 283 to 246 B.C. Around 280 B.C., he ordered construction of the Pharos. It was an important part of his plan to revitalize Egypt's economy by increasing trade with other countries. Greek architect Sostratus designed the structure. Workers completed the lighthouse in 247 B.C., immediately following the end of Ptolemy II's time in power. The light guided cargo-laden merchant ships through the harbor of Alexandria.

An earthquake destroyed the lighthouse in the fourteenth century A.D., so we have little accurate information about its construction. Some accounts indicate that the Pharos towered to a height of 600 feet (183 m)—as high as a sixty-story skyscraper. Others put the height at 350 feet (107 m). It was built of stone, with a square base, an octagonal (eight-sided) midsection, and a round upper tower. A light in the tower burned so brightly that sailors reportedly could see

▼ This seventeenth-century drawing shows what the Pharos of Alexandria might have looked like. This lighthouse is known as one of the Seven Wonders of the Ancient World. It lit the way for sailors along the Egyptian coast of the Mediterranean Sea.

it from 30 miles (48 km) away. Experts are unsure what materials lighthouse tenders burned in the lighthouse, but wood is the most likely answer.

The tower became so famous that *pharos* came to mean "lighthouse" in Greek and many other languages. The word is *faro* in Italian and *phare* in French. People who study lighthouse construction are called pharologists.

TRIREMES

The standard battleship in ancient Greece was a swift boat called the trireme. The trireme was equipped with a heavy front side battering ram for sinking enemy ships. Once a trireme had rammed an enemy ship, sailors boarded the ship and attacked their rivals hand to hand or with swords. A typical trireme was about 140 feet (43 m) long and 20 feet (6 m) wide.

The word *trireme* comes from the Latin *triremis*, which means "having three oars to each bench." The vessels were outfitted with three decks of rowers. Thirty-one men typically occupied the top bank, with twenty-seven in each lower bank.

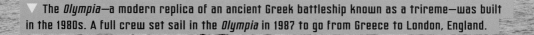

▼ The *Olympia*—a modern replica of an ancient Greek battleship known as a trireme—was built in the 1980s. A full crew set sail in the *Olympia* in 1987 to go from Greece to London, England.

Triremes evolved from the Phoenician bireme, an earlier, smaller vessel. It had two decks of rowers. According to the ancient Greek historian Thucydides, the people of Corinth, a Greek city-state, designed the first trireme around the seventh century B.C. Triremes gradually evolved into bigger battleships. According to legend, the last of these giant vessels seated thousands of rowers, with up to sixteen men pulling each huge oar.

ANCIENT FREIGHTERS

Alexandria was an important ancient trade center. Hundreds of merchant ships sailed trade routes to and from the city at the mouth of the Nile. The ships were laden with wine, olive oil, corn, wheat, fruit, timber, fabrics, dyes, hides, live animals, and a tremendous assortment of other goods.

Shipping costs were determined by the same factors twenty-three hundred years ago as they are in modern times. A key factor was the amount of cargo on a ship. Big ships transporting lots of cargo were more cost-effective than multiple smaller ships. Most Greek cargo ships could hold 150 tons (136 metric tons) of freight. The standard Greek grain ship carried 340 tons (308

> "[W]hat a size that ship was! 180 feet [55 m] long . . . and something over a quarter of that in width; and from deck to keep, the maximum depth, through the hold, 44 feet [13 m]. . . . The crew was like a small army. And they were saying she carried as much corn as would feed every soul in Attica [ancient district of east central Greece] for a year."

—Lucian, Greek writer, on the freighter *Isis*, a 1,228-ton (1,114-metric-ton) ship, second century A.D.

metric tons). Some ships carried even more. By contrast, caravels, the most advanced ships built in fifteenth-century Spain and Portugal, held only about 125 tons (113 metric tons).

A GREEK SEA MONSTER

No ancient cargo ship matched the size of the *Syracusia*. King Hieron II of the Greek city of Syracuse ordered this ship built around 250 B.C. We don't know the *Syracusia*'s exact dimensions. But a historian of the time, Moschion, wrote of the ship's massive size. He described the enormous quantities of food and goods on board. Based on Moschion's account, modern-day researchers have calculated that the *Syracusia* may have carried a cargo of around 2,000 tons (1,814 metric tons).

The *Syracusia* was lavishly equipped. It transported 20,000 gallons (75,708 liters) of freshwater and wooden tanks of seawater filled with live fish. It had a stable for horses, a kitchen with stoves and ovens, storerooms for food and other provisions, and even a gymnasium.

Like many other trading vessels, the *Syracusia* was heavily armed for protection against pirates. It reportedly had its own catapult and a supply of large rocks for ammunition. The ship carried a guard of at least two hundred marines.

Greek ships were built to carry a lot of cargo and withstand storms—but not necessarily for speed. Even with favorable winds billowing their sails, most Greek freighters could travel at only about 6 knots—about 7 miles (11 km) per hour.

BOAT BRIDGES

Some experts believe that boat bridges—chains of boats tied together to span rivers—were the first long bridges. Boat bridges allowed people to move back and forth between two bodies of land without sailing in between them. Armies often used boat bridges because they could be built quickly. The Greek historian Herodotus, who lived from 484 to 425 B.C., wrote several accounts of these bridges. One comes from his account of the wars between Greece and Persia in the fifth century B.C.:

> The men assigned to this grotesque task carried out their orders. . . . They made a solid wall of penteconters [another type of Greek ship] and triremes, 360 of them to support the bridge on the side nearest the Euxine Sea [Black Sea] and 314 on the other side. Once they had the boats all massed together, they let down anchors . . . on both sides—from the pontoon [small flat-bottomed boat] on the Euxine side to counteract the winds blowing from within the Euxine, and from the westward, Aegean [in the Mediterranean Sea, east of Greece] pontoon to counteract the winds from the west and south.

Bridge builders such as the people Herodotus describes often left gaps between ships at water level to allow small boats to pass through. But these bridges were still an effective means of crossing wide bodies of water.

AN ANCIENT OWNER'S MANUAL

Horses were essential for transportation in the ancient world. They also were critical weapons. A horse's performance

▼ Horses were key weapons in ancient battles, and the Greeks were master horsemen. This relief carving from the fourth-century B.C. tomb of Alexander the Great shows Alexander *(right)* fighting the Persian army.

▲ This statue of Xenophon—who wrote the world's first horse-training book—stands outside the parliament building in Vienna, Austria.

often meant the difference between life and death in battle. Ancient peoples thus were eager for advice on the proper care and handling of these valuable animals.

A Greek cavalryman named Xenophon wrote the world's first manual on the training and care of horses. It was titled *The Art of Horsemanship.* Xenophon lived from around 430 to around 355 B.C. Much of his advice remains the best available, even after almost twenty-five hundred years. In this insightful passage, Xenophon urges horse owners to maintain a calm temperament:

Never deal with [your horse] when you are in a fit of passion. When your horse shies at an object and is unwilling to go up to it, he should be shown there is nothing fearful in it, least of all to a courageous horse like him. But if this fails, touch the object yourself that seems so dreadful to him, and lead him up to it with gentleness. Compulsion and blows inspire only the more fear; and when horses are at all hurt at such times, they think what they shied at is the cause of the hurt.

EARTH IS ROUND!

The Babylonians of Mesopotamia were great mapmakers. Over time, Babylonians introduced valuable map elements such as cardinal points (north, south, east, and west) and scales that related distance on a map to

THE FIRST MARATHON

The Greeks didn't do all their travel by sea. On land, running was one of the fastest ways of transporting messages. Kings, politicians, and generals used runners to send information. Greek legend tells of the most famous message ever delivered by foot. It was sent during the Persian Wars (499–449 B.C.). A Persian army landed at the Greek city of Marathon, about 25 miles (40 m) north of Athens. It was defeated by a small Greek force from the city of Athens. The Greeks wanted to get news of the victory to Athens as quickly as possible. According to the legend, they turned to their fastest runner, who had just returned from a 150-mile (241 km) trip to the city-state of Sparta. He took the assignment nonetheless, reached Athens, cried out, "Rejoice, we are victorious," and dropped dead of exhaustion *(above, in a modern illustration)*. The modern marathon, 26 miles (42 km), 385 yards (352 m), is named in honor of his remarkable run.

actual distances on Earth. From that base of knowledge, the Greeks made several technological leaps in mapping.

Most historians are convinced that Greek scholars were the first to realize that Earth is round rather than flat. Some trace the idea of a round Earth to Pythagoras, a Greek mathematician who lived from 580 to 500 B.C. Others think the idea originated with Parmenides, a Greek philosopher born around 515 B.C. In approximately 350 B.C., the Greek philosopher Aristotle developed six arguments for a round Earth. He noted, for instance, that travelers saw different constellations depending on where they were stationed. On a flat Earth, travelers would have seen the same constellations as they moved from place to place.

BASICS OF NAVIGATION

Sea travel greatly depends on a sailor's ability to figure out the position and the course of a ship. Finding a specific position requires knowing a set of points called latitude and longitude.

Latitude is distance north or south of the equator, a horizontal line tracing Earth's center at equal distances from the North Pole and the South Pole. It is measured in units called degrees. Each degree of latitude is about 69 miles (111 km). Longitude is distance east or west of the prime meridian, a line running from the North Pole to the South Pole through Greenwich, England. At the equator, each degree of longitude also equals 69 miles (111 km).

The use of latitude and longitude to identify points on a map originated around 300 B.C. Working with a map of the world, a Greek scholar named Dicaearchus drew a latitude line that extended east and west through Rhodes (in Greece) and Gibraltar (in Spain). Other scholars later expanded upon Dicaearchus's concept. They added lines of longitude to maps.

BETTER MAPMAKERS

Many ancient maps were based on stories from travelers and soldiers. Few mapmakers actually traveled, saw land features firsthand, or made their own diagrams and notes. Sometimes features on their maps were based on legends and travelers' tales.

Herodotus was an exception. He visited many countries and accurately recorded geographic details. When he compared his own personal knowledge with the maps he saw, Herodotus had one response:

> I am amused when I see that not one of all the people who have drawn maps of the world has set it out sensibly. They show Ocean as a river flowing around the outside of the earth, which is as circular as if it had been drawn with a pair of compasses, and they make Asia and Europe the same size.

Herodotus drew his own map of the world. His map represented countries, bodies of water, cities, and other geographical features more accurately.

One of the greatest innovators in mapmaking was Ptolemy. This Egyptian astronomer and scholar lived in Alexandria in the second century A.D. (He was most likely not related to Ptolemy II or other Greek rulers who bore the same name.) He wrote a massive, eight-volume, Greek-language book called *Geographia* (*Geography*). It included the most accurate map of the world to that point in history. The map identified more than eight thousand places and listed their latitude and longitude.

Ptolemy's map was the basis for all world maps produced in Europe for the next thirteen hundred years. When Ptolemy's book was translated into Latin in A.D. 1406, it helped people realize the extent and the nature of the world. Ptolemy's map did contain errors. For instance, it underestimated the size of Earth. It depicted Europe and Asia as spanning half the globe.

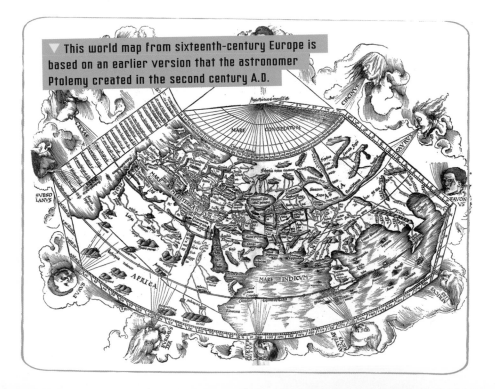

This world map from sixteenth-century Europe is based on an earlier version that the astronomer Ptolemy created in the second century A.D.

CHAPTER EIGHT

ANCIENT ROME

Rome was a great military power of the ancient world. From their base in present-day Italy, the Romans conquered many other countries and developed an empire. At its height, the Roman Empire stretched through much of Europe, northern Africa, and parts of the Middle East.

The Roman military needed a fast, reliable means of transporting armies, supplies, and messages to distant parts of the empire. To fill that need, Rome built the ancient world's greatest highway system.

▼ This section of Trajan's Column in Rome, Italy, shows Roman cavalry crossing a wooden bridge. Efficient transportation was key to the Roman army's success. Romans erected the column between A.D. 106 and 113.

WOODEN ROADS

Rome's first paved roads were made from wood. To lay the foundation of these roads, engineers cut wedge-shaped boards from oak or alder trees. They placed these boards angled-side down for greater stability. They set paving boards on top and fastened them with wooden stakes. The thick edge of one paving board covered the thin edge of the next.

The Romans also built elevated wooden roads over soft or swampy ground. Road builders pounded long stakes into the soil. Some stakes were 7 feet (2.1 m) long. The ends rose above the surface to a uniform height. Workers covered the tops of the stakes with boards. A layer of gravel served as pavement.

These wooden roads proved to be remarkably durable. Segments of the Roman roads, some 13 feet (4 m) wide, can still be found in parts of Europe.

ROADS BUILT TO LAST

The most durable Roman roads were made of layers of packed earth, stone blocks, sand, and other materials. Some roads were 5 feet (1.5 m) thick. They were paved with blocks of cut stone or rocks mixed with cementlike material.

Roads through rainy areas had a cambered, or arched, surface. These roads were higher in the center than at the sides. This shape allowed water to drain off the surface, so it would not soak into the road and damage it. (Modern roads still have this cambered design.) Most Roman roads had curbstones and drainage ditches at the sides. Stretches of road through towns had elevated sidewalks, so pedestrians could walk at a safe distance from draft animals and wheeled carts.

Many ancient civilizations, including the Mesopotamians, Egyptians, Indians, Chinese, and Greeks, built paved roads for the military. But none matched the system of roads begun in 312 B.C. by the Roman politician Appius Claudius Caecus.

Appius Claudius's system included more than 370 major roads. The system extended across about 50,000 miles (80,467 km). It connected all the large towns of the Roman territories—from Greece to Spain to Scotland. At every thousand paces (about 0.9 miles, or 1.5 km), markers along the roads told troops how far they had traveled.

The oldest and most famous Roman road was the Via Appia, or Appian Way. It went south from the Servian Wall in the city of Rome to the city of Capua in southern Italy. The road was more than 350 miles (563 km) long and 35 feet (11 m) wide.

Like many other Roman roads, the Appian Way was built as straight as possible. Although a straight line is the shortest distance between two towns, straight lines were an important aspect of Roman road design for another reason. Roman wagons had fixed axles. They could not move to steer the vehicle. Wagons could travel only straight, so roads had to follow. To get a wagon off a road, workers had to inch it to the curb with huge pry bars.

▼ Roman workers built the Appian Way in the fourth century B.C. It connected Rome to southern Italy. This section is in Rome, Italy.

ANCIENT TRAFFIC LAWS

Even in ancient times, vehicles created traffic jams, especially in the city of Rome. At times, oxcarts, chariots, handcarts, mounted horses, and farm wagons were barely able to move along the congested roads. The Roman Senate enacted traffic laws. It set up stop signs, one-way streets, and parking places. But these laws didn't solve the problem. Finally, ruler Julius Caesar, who lived from about 100 to 44 B.C., enacted the Lex Julia Municipalis. This law banned certain vehicles from city streets in the daytime.

ROAD SERVICE

The Roman government had an official courier service called the *cursus publicus* (public course). It delivered mail throughout the territories. Couriers traveled on horseback as quickly as possible. When horses became exhausted, couriers could get new ones at posts along the roads. Posts stood along roadways every 10 miles (16 km). Each post had large stables of horses and attendants, including veterinarians.

Roman roads also had roadhouses where travelers could buy a meal, sleep, and rest their horses. Government officials and wealthy businesspeople stayed at elaborate roadhouses called *mansiones*. They were stationed about

"Appia teritur regina longarum viarum [The Appian Way is commonly said to be the queen of the long roads]."

—Publius Papinius Statius, Roman writer, *Silvae*, first century A.D.

In this ancient Roman relief, travelers stop at a roadhouse. Roadhouses offered food, beds, and stables.

every 19 miles (30 km) along roads. Public roadhouses served ordinary travelers. They were dangerous places where guests were sometimes robbed. Many travelers preferred to stay with friends or relatives instead.

ROMAN TRAVEL GUIDES

Ancient Roman travelers used guides called *itineraria* (from the Latin word *itinerari*, meaning "to travel"). They were similar to modern-day packets of maps and travel brochures. Itineraria were written on parchment (sheets made from animal hide) or papyrus. The guides showed the location of famous tombs and other sightseeing attractions, as well as roadhouses, bridges, rivers, and other features along roads. Itineraria sometimes mentioned areas of construction. They mainly focused on problems of greater concern to ancient travelers, such as hungry wolves on a path.

Experts believe that the master source for many itineraria may have been the Peutinger Table. This parchment scroll showed all the roads of the Roman Empire, from the Middle East to Britain. The table showed the location of roadhouses and bathhouses. It listed distances and the most

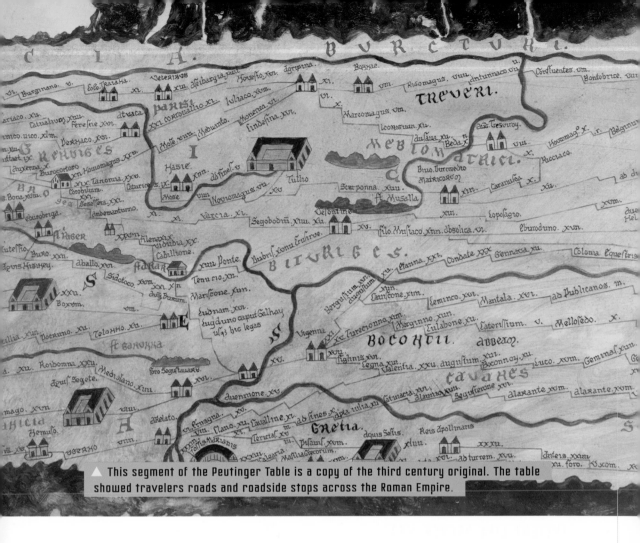

▲ This segment of the Peutinger Table is a copy of the third century original. The table showed travelers roads and roadside stops across the Roman Empire.

efficient routes between towns. The Peutinger Table in turn probably was based on a map of the world drawn by Marcus Agrippa, a Roman general who lived from 63 to 12 B.C.

WARSHIPS

For centuries Rome controlled the Mediterranean Sea. It built many warships to maintain its power. Some ships had catapults for hurling stones at enemies and pirates. Other ships had movable bridges that allowed soldiers to board enemy vessels.

The *dromon* was the greatest Roman warship. The Roman Empire used the dromon after the fourth century A.D. This swift vessel had sails, banks of

This mosaic shows a Roman galley, or warship powered by rowers. An artist created the mosaic between the first and third centuries.

rowers, and tough armor made from leather and cloth. The armor was soaked with vinegar and other fluids. These liquids kept ships from catching on fire when hit by hot stones or flaming arrows.

ANCIENT LIFE PRESERVERS

The inflated sheepskins that people in Mesopotamia used as water floats worked well, but they had a big disadvantage. Even with the most skillful construction, they constantly lost air from their seams. They frequently had to be reinflated.

The ancient Romans introduced a "swimming belt" that improved on Mesopotamian float technology. The belt was a leather tube filled with cork, which comes from oak trees. Cork is very light and floats on water. A poor swimmer could use the swimming belt to cross a river or survive a shipwreck. The first record of a Roman swimming belt dates to 390 B.C. It describes a military messenger who used a swimming belt to reach Rome by crossing the Tiber River.

THE PORT OF COSA

The port of Cosa, north of Rome on the Mediterranean coast, was one of the Roman Empire's most important cultural centers and trading hubs. At its peak, around 100 B.C., Cosa made, packaged, and shipped two main products: wine and dried, salted fish. Both items were mainstays of the Roman diet.

Cosa had its own fish farming operation. This included a huge natural lagoon and about 43,500 square feet (4,000 sq. m) of concrete fish tanks. According to archaeologists, the tanks alone could have yielded 3.3 million pounds (1.5 million kg) of fish each year.

A breakwater, a wall of limestone blocks, protected the vessels docked at Cosa from incoming waves. Two piers for loading and unloading ships stood on the Cosa breakwater. Three more were nearby on concrete piles. Evidence suggests that Cosa also had a lighthouse that was more than 90 feet (27 m) high.

▼ In modern times, only ruins remain of the port of Cosa on Italy's west coast. Cosa was known in the ancient Roman Empire as a busy trading hub.

AFTER THE ANCIENTS

Ancient civilizations rose and fell. Often civilizations grew politically or economically weak, and stronger groups conquered them. But even after a civilization died out, its technology often remained. Conquering groups built on the knowledge of conquered peoples to further develop technology.

This wasn't always the case, however. After the Roman Empire fell to invaders in A.D. 476, Europe entered a period called the Middle Ages (about 500 to 1500). The early Middle Ages are sometimes called the Dark Ages, because art, culture, and learning did not flourish in Europe during these years. Few people in Europe went to school. Few craftspeople knew about or improved upon ancient technology.

IN THE DARK

After the Roman Empire collapsed, Roman roads began to deteriorate because no one maintained them. Even so, they remained the best roads in Europe for centuries. Not a single new highway was built in Europe for more than five hundred years after Rome fell.

Progress in mapmaking slowed during Europe's Middle Ages. Few original ancient maps survived this period. In modern times, we only have copies of most ancient maps. We don't know how accurately early scholars followed the originals. It's possible that each scholar added personal artistic touches.

Advances in transportation did not stop completely during the Middle Ages. For instance, Europeans began using the wheelbarrow around the twelfth century. During this time, workers built many large cathedrals. Wheelbarrows allowed them to more efficiently haul heavy building materials.

This fourteenth-century Dutch illustration shows a man using a wheelbarrow. The Chinese developed this tool sometime before 200 B.C. European workers did not use wheelbarrows until the twelfth century A.D.

Europeans also learned more about ancient boat making. In the late 1200s and early 1300s, Italian traveler Marco Polo sailed to central Asia and China. In 1298 he praised the Chinese bulkhead system for its stability. Polo noted that even if a ship "springs a leak by running against a rock, or on being hit by a hungry whale," bulkheads prevent it from sinking. Surprisingly, European boatbuilders didn't adopt bulkheads until the nineteenth century.

INVENTION AND DISCOVERY

In the 1300s, Europeans took a renewed interest in learning, literature, art, and technology. Europe entered a period of creative outpouring called the Renaissance (1300s–1600). The name *Renaissance* means "rebirth."

Leonardo da Vinci (1452–1519) was a gifted Italian painter, sculptor, mathematician, and inventor. He produced some of the first known designs for flying machines. The machines were never built in Leonardo's lifetime. Some wouldn't have been able to actually fly. But the designs influenced future generations. One resembles a motorless helicopter and another a hang glider.

Leonardo may have been inspired by an earlier mind. According to second century A.D. Roman writer Aulus Gellius, the Greek mathematician Archytas developed a bird-shaped flying craft during the 300s B.C. The craft, called the *Pigeon*, reportedly traveled across short distances while suspended on a wire.

THE AGE OF DISCOVERY

The Renaissance coincided with an era known as the Age of Discovery. Throughout the fifteenth and sixteenth centuries, explorers from Europe traveled the sea in search of rare goods and new trade routes. For many

▲ This page from one of Leonardo da Vinci's notebooks (dating to 1480) shows one of his many drawings of flying machines. He called this design a helical air screw.

European nations, the Age of Discovery marked the start of regular contact with Asia and Africa. The era also marked the first European visits to North and South America.

In the 1400s, Middle Eastern traders learned about the compass from the Chinese. Compass technology soon spread to Europe. This tool helped make possible such sea voyages as Christopher Columbus's trips to the New World (North and South America). Columbus, an Italian explorer working for Spain, arrived in the Americas in 1492. He had been sailing west across the Atlantic, looking for a new route to India. Columbus used maps based on Ptolemy's designs, which did not include the Americas.

The Age of Discovery encouraged advances in mapping and navigation. By the eighteenth century, Europeans had an improved map of the world. It reflected the shapes of continents and distances between them much more closely than previous attempts.

THE INDUSTRIAL REVOLUTION

In the mid-1700s, Europe entered an era known as the Industrial Revolution. During this period, improvements in power-driven machines allowed people to produce goods more quickly and in larger amounts than they could by hand. Across Europe, large factories opened. Many people moved from farms to cities.

Changes in the way people made goods demanded new ways to transport goods and the materials used to make them. Engineers developed new ways to pave roads, such as laying down thin layers of crushed rock. The new roads were smoother, and vehicles traveled across them more quickly. In 1769 Scottish engineer James Watt perfected the steam engine. Watt's invention soon powered both vehicles and factory machinery.

In 1804 British engineer Richard Trevithick built the first steam locomotive, an engine-powered vehicle designed for railways. Workers built and laid thousands of miles of railroad track. In 1807 U.S. inventor Robert Fulton built a practical steam-powered boat. Fulton's boat was able to

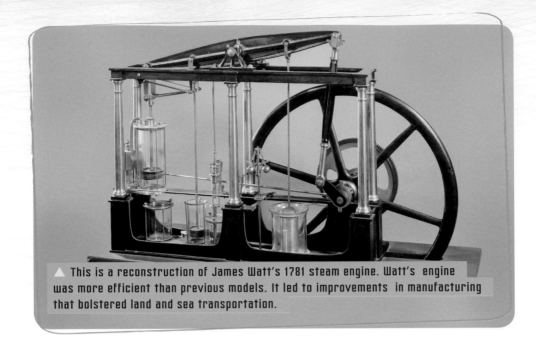

▲ This is a reconstruction of James Watt's 1781 steam engine. Watt's engine was more efficient than previous models. It led to improvements in manufacturing that bolstered land and sea transportation.

travel much faster than most boats without engines. Within a few decades, steamboats traveled between the United States and Europe.

CHANGES ON LAND AND IN THE AIR

For centuries after the Renaissance, people continued to think about flight. In 1783 French inventors created the first flying balloons capable of carrying human passengers. In the 1800s, several inventors in the United States and Europe built gliders, crafts that could fly short distances on wind currents. Motor-powered flight craft emerged by the early 1900s following innovations from American inventors Wilbur and Orville Wright and others. A couple of decades later, people were producing airplanes on a massive scale.

Meanwhile, the motor-powered automobile arrived. As with flying machines, no single person is responsible for the automobile. In 1885 German inventor Karl Benz built the first wheeled vehicle to run solely on gasoline. In 1908 U.S. inventor Henry Ford designed the Model T, the first automobile that most middle-class Americans could afford. Ford also devised assembly lines, a way for factories to quickly produce large numbers of automobiles. The work of Benz, Ford, and others depended on many ancient innovations, such as wheels joined by axles and tires made from multiple parts.

The automobile led to the creation of modern highway systems. From road signs to rest stops to the organizations needed to maintain them, modern highways have much in common with the roadways of ancient Rome and

German inventor Karl Benz and his assistant pose in his 1885 Benz Motorwagen—an early automobile. Many experts consider the motorwagen to be the first practical automobile.

ancient India. Parts of the Appian Way are also still in use. They carry car and truck traffic after more than twenty-three hundred years.

LOOKING BACKWARD

Some of the most popular modern means of transportation, such as cars, buses, and airplanes, may not resemble the popular vehicles of ancient times—even if these modern vehicles rely on the innovations of early peoples. But some forms of transportation remain the same hundreds of years after they were invented. The modern wheelbarrow shares its basic design with the wheelbarrow of ancient China. Modern skis and snowshoes likewise take the same shapes as their ancient versions. These items are still some of the most effective means of traveling over snowy ground.

Some modern people work to re-create the transportation technology of ancient cultures. In 1987 a group of historians and architects called the Trireme Trust oversaw the building of a full-size warship in the style of the Greek trireme. The group took the ship on several test voyages. By constructing its own trireme, the Trireme Trust learned more about how quickly Greek ships could move and how much power it took to move them.

TIMELINE

CA. 10,000 B.C.	People begin to form permanent villages and domesticate animals.
CA. 4000 B.C.	People in the Middle East tame wild horses.
CA. 3000 B.C.	The Phoenicians introduce sails on their *gauli*.
CA. 2000 B.C.	Riding on horseback becomes popular in the Middle East. Inventors in Mesopotamia develop the spoked wheel.
CA. 1700 B.C.	The Hittites begin riding horse-drawn chariots in battle.
CA. 1400 B.C.	Egyptian woodworkers make wheels with separate rims, spokes, and hubs.
CA. 1350 B.C.	Hittite cavalryman Kikkuli writes the first systematic plan for raising a chariot horse.
1200S B.C.	Egyptian engineers dig a canal that allows ships to pass from the Mediterranean Sea to the Red Sea.
	Persian king Darius I orders the building of a waterway to the Red Sea and an extensive roadway system.
486 B.C.	Construction begins on China's Grand Canal.
312 B.C.	Appius Claudius Caecus conceives a system of roads across the Roman Empire.
CA. 300 B.C.	Greek astronomer Dicaearchus begins the practice of including latitude lines on maps. Indian horse riders begin using stirrups.
280 B.C.	Greek ruler Ptolemy II orders the construction of the Pharos of Alexandria.
250 B.C.	King Hieron II of Syracuse orders the building of a massive freighter the *Syracusia*.
A.D. 476	The Roman Empire falls to invaders.
500	Europe enters the Middle Ages.
1300S	Europe enters the Renaissance.

1400S	The Age of Discovery begins.
1500S	European explorers begin regular travel to the Americas.
1700S	The Age of Discovery comes to a close, and the Industrial Revolution begins.
1769	Scottish inventor James Watt perfects the steam engine.
1804	British inventor Richard Trevithick builds the first steam locomotive.
1807	American engineer Robert Fulton builds the first commercially successful steam-powered boat.
1885	German engineer Karl Benz builds the first wheeled vehicle to run solely on gasoline.
1908	American industrialist Henry Ford designs the Model T.
1987	The Trireme Trust oversees the building of a full-size Greek trireme. They sail it to learn more about the practicality, maneuverability, and speed of the ancient trireme.
2009	Archaeologists on the island of Crete discover ancient stone tools that raise questions about the earliest dates of extended boat travel.
2010	Archaeologists in Armenia discover the world's oldest known leather shoe.

GLOSSARY

ARCHAEOLOGIST: a scientist who studies the remains of past human cultures

ARTIFACT: a human-made object, especially one characteristic of a certain group or historical period

AXLE: a rod in the center of a wheel

BARGE: a long boat with a flat bottom

BULKHEAD: a solid wall on the body of a boat made from wooden planks

CANAL: a channel that is dug across land to connect bodies of water

CANOE: a narrow boat powered by paddling

CARDINAL POINTS: the four principal compass points—north, south, east, and west

CAVALRY: soldiers who fight on horseback

CHARIOT: a small wheeled vehicle pulled by one or more horses

COMPASS: a device with a magnetic needle that is used to determine direction

CUNEIFORM: a writing technique that involves making wedge-shaped signs or letters on a surface

DOMESTICATE: to adapt an animal or a plant for human use

GALLEY: a boat powered by rowers

HUNTER-GATHERERS: people who obtain their food by hunting, fishing, and gathering wild plants

JUNK: a boxy Chinese ship with a flat bottom, a high rear, and a low front

KELEK: an Assyrian raft made from inflated sheepskins under a wooden frame

LATITUDE: a measurement of distance north or south of Earth's equator

LONGITUDE: a measurement of distance east or west of Earth's prime meridian

MASTODON: extinct animals of the elephant family

MASULA: an Indian boat or group of boats with planks and frames bound by rope

MESOAMERICA: the area extending from Mexico south to the Isthmus of Panama before the arrival of European settlers

NAVIGATION: travel by a map, a compass, or other guide

OUTRIGGER: a ship with a beam extending from its side to support a central mast

PORT: a place where boats and ships can dock

PRIME MERIDIAN: a line running from the North Pole to the South Pole through Greenwich, England

RAFT: a floating platform made from bound logs

RELIEF: a sculpture featuring raised forms and figures on a flat surface

RUDDER: a large underwater plate at the back of a boat or a ship, used for steering

SILK ROAD: an ancient trade route that extended from China to the Mediterranean Sea

SLEDGE: a flat vehicle such as a sleigh, used to drag objects across the ground

STIRRUP: a loop that hangs from a horse's saddle into which a rider places his feet for balance and ease of mounting

TRAVOIS: a vehicle consisting of two poles and sometimes an attached sled, dragged by a person or an animal across the ground

TRIREME: a Greek battleship, typically with three banks of rowers

YOKE: a pole carried across the shoulder, used to transport items

SOURCE NOTES

16   John George Wood, *The Natural History of Man*, vol. 2 (London: George Routledge and Sons, 1870), 103.

21   Herodotus, *The Histories*, trans. Robin Waterfield (Oxford: Oxford University Press, 1998), 85.

24   "Harnessing the Horse: Kikkuli, 1345 B.C.E.: Training the Chariot Horse," International Museum of the Horse, http://imh.org/legacy-of-the-horse/kikkuli-1345 (July 15, 2010).

33   Andrew Robert Burn, *Persia and the Greeks: The Defence of the West, c. 546–478 B.C.* 2nd ed. (Stanford, CA: Stanford University Press, 1984), 115.

38   Kerry S. Walters and Lisa Portmess, eds., *Religious Vegetarianism* (Albany: State University of New York Press, 2001), 75.

48   Nathaniel Hawthorne, *The Complete Works of Nathaniel Hawthorne*, vol. 7 (Boston: Houghton, Mifflin and Co, 1883), 38.

50   Joseph Needham, *Science and Civilisation in China*, vol. 4 (Cambridge: Cambridge University Press, 1954), 262.

51   Amir D. Aczel, *The Riddle of the Compass: The Invention That Changed the World* (New York: Harcourt, 2001), 80.

55   Gary E. Moulton, ed., *The Definitive Journals of Lewis and Clark* (Lincoln: University of Nebraska Press, 2002), 284.

63   Lucian of Samosata, *The Works of Lucian of Samosata*, vol. 4, trans. Henry Watson Fowler and Francis George Fowler (Oxford, UK: Clarendon Press, 1905), 35.

65   Herodotus, 420.

66   Xenophon, *The Art of Horsemanship*, trans. Morris H. Morgan (London: J. A. Allen, 1962), 37.

68 Herodotus, 247.

73 John August Hare, *Walks in Rome* (New York: Macmillan, 1903), 297.

79 Thomas Ask, *Handbook of Marine Surveying* (Dobbs Ferry, NY: Sheridan House, 2007), 109.

SELECTED BIBLIOGRAPHY

Aust, Siegfried. *Ships! Come Aboard.* Minneapolis: Lerner Publications Company, 1993.

Barbieri-Low, Anthony. "Wheeled Vehicles in the Chinese Bronze Age (c. 2000–741 B.C.)." *Sino-Platonic Papers* 99 (February 2000): 1–98.

Bunch, Bryan H., and Alexander Hellemans. *The Timetables of Technology: A Chronology of the Most Important People and Events in the History of Technology.* New York: Simon & Schuster, 1993.

Casson, Lionel. *Ships and Seamanship in the Ancient World.* Baltimore: Johns Hopkins University Press, 1995.

Cotterell, Arthur. *China's Civilization: A Survey of Its History, Arts and Technology.* New York: Praeger, 1975.

De Bono, Edward. *Eureka! How and When the Greatest Inventions Were Made.* New York: Holt, Rinehart, and Winston, 1974.

Dilke, O. A. W. *The Ancient Romans: How They Lived and Worked.* Chester Springs, PA: Dufour Editions, 1975.

Gardiner, Robert, ed. *The Earliest Ships: The Evolution of Boats into Ships.* Annapolis, MD: Naval Institute Press, 1996.

Humble, Richard. *Ships: Sailors and the Sea.* New York: Franklin Watts, 1991.

James, Peter, and Nick Thorpe. *Ancient Inventions.* New York: Ballantine, 1994.

Johnstone, Paul. *The Seacraft of Prehistory.* Cambridge, MA: Harvard University Press, 1980.

Kerrod, Robin. *Transportation: From the Bicycle to Spacecraft.* New York: Macmillan, 1991.

"Legacy of the Horse." International Museum of the Horse. December 8 1998. http://imh.org/legacy-of-the-horse/ (August 19, 2010).

Neuberger, Albert. *The Technical Arts and Sciences of the Ancients.* New York: Barnes & Noble, 1969.

Perry, Marvin. *A History of the Ancient World.* Boston: Houghton Mifflin, 1985.

Saggs, H. W. F. *Civilization Before Greece and Rome.* New Haven, CT: Yale University Press, 1989.

Starr, Chester G., Jr., ed. *A History of the Ancient World.* New York: Oxford University Press, 1991.

White, K. D. *Greek and Roman Technology.* Ithaca, NY: Cornell University Press, 1984.

Wilkinson, Philip, ed. *Early Humans.* New York: Knopf, 1989.

FURTHER READING

Behnke, Alison. *The Conquests of Alexander the Great.* Minneapolis: Twenty-First Century Books, 2008. Alexander the Great founded the famous city of Alexandria, Egypt, home to the Pharos of Alexandria. This book describes his life and achievements.

Childress, Diana. *Marco Polo's Journey to China.* Minneapolis: Twenty-First Century Books, 2008. Learn more about Italian merchant Marco Polo's visit to China and the records he kept of his travels.

Chrisp, Peter. *Atlas of Ancient Worlds.* New York: DK Publishing, 2009. This book highlights several different ancient societies and features maps, illustrations, and a CD with additional content.

Dickinson, Rachel. *Tools of Navigation: A Kid's Guide to the History and Science of Finding Your Way*. White River Junction, VT: Nomad Press, 2005. Check out this book for information, diagrams, and activities about navigational tools of the ancient and modern world.

Fields, Nic. *Ancient Greek Warship: 500–322 B.C.* Oxford, UK: Osprey Publishing, 2007. Find out more about the Greek trireme, such as how the ship was built and major sea battles the Greeks fought with this mighty vessel.

Galloway, Priscilla, and Dawn Hunter. *Adventures on the Ancient Silk Road*. Toronto, ON: Annick Press, 2009. This book describes the journeys of three different historical figures along China's Silk Road, including Marco Polo and the warrior Genghis Khan.

Kirkpatrick, Naida. *The Indus Valley*. Chicago: Heinemann Library, 2002. This book examines the growth of ancient India's Indus River valley civilization.

Passport to History series. Minneapolis: Twenty-First Century Books, 2001–2004. In this series, readers will take trips back in time to ancient China, Egypt, Greece, Rome, and the Mayan civilization. They will learn about people's clothing, transportation, buildings, and other aspects of daily life.

Perl, Lila. *The Ancient Maya*. New York: Franklin Watts, 2005. This title examines ancient Mayan life and culture.

Woods, Michael, and Mary B. Woods. *Seven Wonders of the Ancient World*. Minneapolis: Twenty-First Century Books, 2009. This is one of seven books in a series that gives readers a tour of amazing monuments from throughout the ancient world. Each book focuses on the landmarks and innovations of a different region.

Visual Geography Series. Minneapolis: Twenty-First Century Books, 2003–2011. Each book in this series examines one country, with information about its ancient history. The companion website, vgsbooks.com, offers additional free, downloadable information about each country.

WEBSITES

DISCOVERY CHANNEL: ANCIENT SHIPS

http://www.yourdiscovery.com/ships/ancient_ships/

This site from the Discovery Channel has photos of and information about ancient ships such as Greek barges and the Chinese junk.

HISTORY WORLD: HISTORY OF DOMESTICATION OF ANIMALS

http://www.historyworld.net/wrldhis/PlainTextHistories .asp?historyid=ab57

Find out more about how humans came to rely on beasts of burden with this detailed history of the domestication of animals.

NATIONAL GEOGRAPHIC: TOP 10 ANCIENT HIGHWAYS

http://travel.nationalgeographic.com/travel/top-10/ancient-highways/

This site from *National Geographic* magazine lists ten famous transportation routes from before the invention of the automobile.

PHOENICIANS: ANCIENT SHIPS AND SEA TRADE

http://www.phoenician.org/ancient_ships.htm

Learn more about the influential boat-making techniques of the ancient Phoenicians.

INDEX

Age of Discovery. *See* Renaissance
airplanes. *See* flying machines
Americas, 52–59; canoes, 54–55; Inca, 59; Maya, 57–58; Mesoamerica, 56–59, North America, 52–53; Olmec, 56
Appian Way, 72, 73, 83
Ashoka, emperor of India, 36, 38
automobiles, 82–83

boats, 10–11; Chinese, 46–47, 48, 79; Egyptian, 29–31; Greek, 62–65; Indian, 41; Mesoamerican, 58; Middle Eastern, 19–21; Roman, 75–76; steam-powered, 81–82
bridges, 12, 59, 70; boat, 64–65; land, 52

canals, 32–34, 44–45, 58
canoes, 11, 54–55, 58
China, 44–51; canals, 44–45; compass, 50–51; junks, 46–47, 48; Silk Road, 49–50; wheelbarrow, 48–49
compass, 50–51, 81
Cosa, port of, 77
cursus publicus, 73

Dark Ages. *See* Middle Ages
domesticated animals (beasts of burden), 16–17. *See also* elephants, horses

Egypt: boats, 29–31; Khufu, 30–31; maps, 32; paved roads, 35; seafaring vessels, 30–31; sledges, 34–35; Suez Canal, 32–34
elephants, 39–41

flying machines, 80, 82

footwear, 9–10, 52, 54. *See also* shoes
freighters, 32, 63–64

gauli (round sailboat), 21
Greece, 60–69; boat bridges, 64–65; first marathon, 67; freighters, 63–64; horses, 65–66; navigation and mapmaking, 66–69; Pharos of Alexandria, 60–62; Ptolemy, 69; triremes, 62–63, 65

Herodotus, 21, 65, 68–69
horses, 22–24, 42–43, 50, 53, 65–66, 73

Inca, 59
India, 36–43; Ashoka, 36, 38; boats, 41; elephants, 39–41; horses, 42–43; roads, 36–38; stirrups, 42–43
Industrial Revolution, 81–82

junks, 46–47, 48

keleks (inflatable boats), 19–20
Khufu (pharaoh), 30–31

mapmaking, 66–69, 78
maps, 4–5, 25, 32, 81. *See also* mapmaking, Peutinger Table
marathon, first, 67
Maya, 57–58
Mediterranean Sea, 18–19, 32, 39, 50, 60, 75, 77
Middle Ages, 78–79
Middle East: Assyrians, 19–20, 23; Babylonians, 25, 66–67; boats, 19–20; first maps, 25; horses, 22–24; Mesopotamia, 18–21, 24, 25, 26;

Phoenicians, 18–19, 21; sails, 21; Sumerians, 18; wheels and axles, 18, 24–27

navigation, 68, 81. *See also* maps
Nile River, 28–29, 33, 34, 35, 63
North America, 52–53

Olmec, 56

Paleo-Indians, 52
Peutinger Table, 74–75
Pharos of Alexandria, 60–62
Phoenicians, 18–19, 21, 63
ports, 29, 58, 77
Ptolemy, 69, 81
pyramids, 34, 35; Great Pyramid, 30–31

Red Sea, 32–34
Renaissance, 79–81
roads, 13–14, 35, 36–39, 57, 81, 82–83; Roman, 71–74, 78. *See also* Silk Road, Royal Road
Rome, 70–77; Appius Claudius Caecus, 71–72; Cosa, 77; *cursus publicus* (courier system), 73; roads, 71–74; swimming belt, 76; traffic laws, 73; warships, 75–76
Royal Road, 36–38

sails, 21, 29, 47
shoes, 9–10; snow, 54, 83. *See also* footwear
Silk Road, 39, 43, 49–50
skis, 15, 83
sledges, 15–16, 34–35

steam engine, 81–82
stirrups, 42–43
Suez Canal, 32–34
Sweet Track, 13
swimming belt, 76

technology: ancient roots, 5, 7; defined, 4–5; transportation, 6–7
traffic laws, 73
travois, 14, 16, 53
triremes, 62–63, 65, 83

Via Appia. *See* Appian Way

warships, 75–76. *See also* boats, triremes
wheelbarrow, 48–49, 78, 83
wheels and axles, 18, 24–27

yokes, 14, 52

ABOUT THE AUTHORS

Michael Woods is a science and medical journalist in Washington, D.C. He has won many national writing awards. Mary B. Woods is a school librarian. Their past books include the fifteen-volume Disasters Up Close series, the seven-volume 7 Wonders of the Ancient World series, and the seven-volume 7 Wonders of the Natural World series. The Woodses have four children. When not writing, reading, or enjoying their grandchildren, the Woodses travel to gather material for future books.

PHOTO ACKNOWLEDGMENTS